AF559288

WILD LIVES

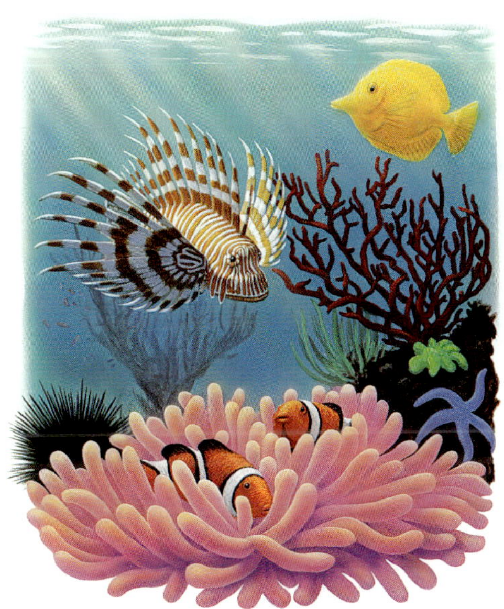

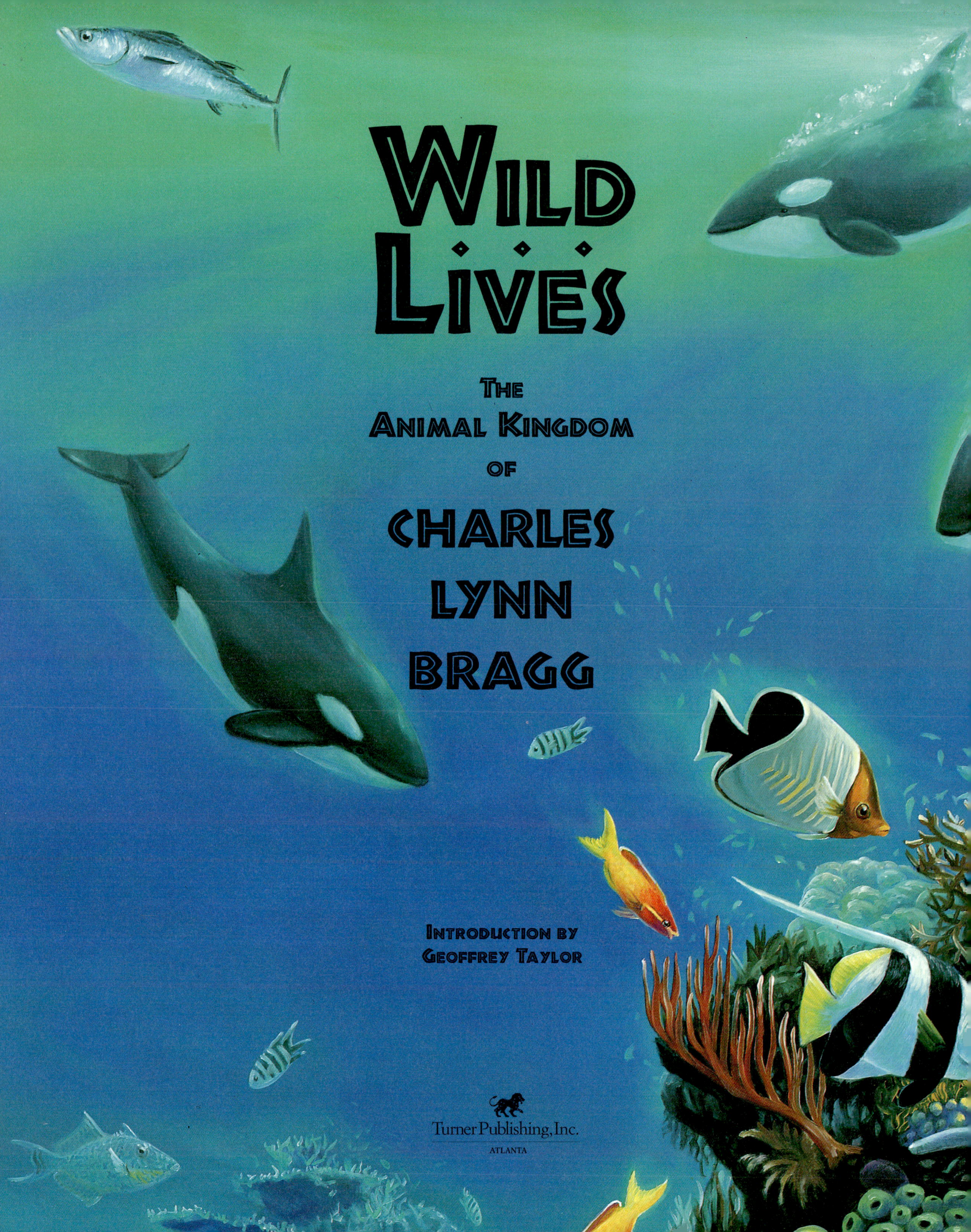

Wild Lives

The Animal Kingdom of Charles Lynn Bragg

Introduction by Geoffrey Taylor

Turner Publishing, Inc.
Atlanta

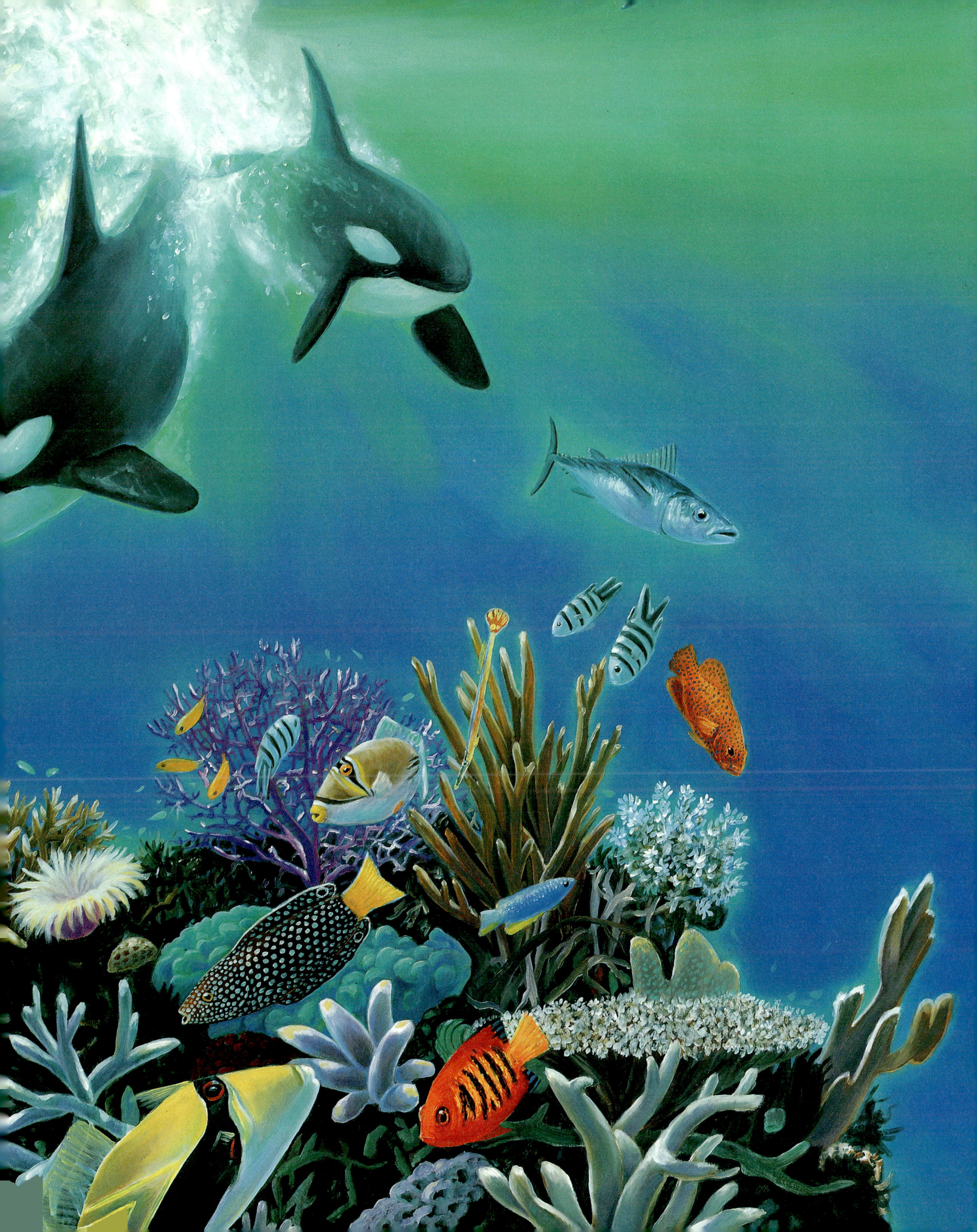

Published by Turner Publishing, Inc.
A Subsidiary of Turner Broadcasting System, Inc.
1050 Techwood Drive, N.W.
Atlanta, Georgia 30318

Distributed by Andrews and McMeel
A Universal Press Syndicate Company
4900 Main Street
Kansas City, Missouri 64112

First Edition 10 9 8 7 6 5 4 3 2 1

Library of Congress Cataloging-in-Publication Data
Bragg, Charles Lynn.
Wild lives: the animal kingdom of Charles Lynn Bragg / introduction by Geoffrey Taylor. — 1st ed.
p. cm.
ISBN 1-57036-065-0
1. Bragg, Charles Lynn—Themes, motives. 2. Wildlife art—United States. I. Title.
N6537.B682A4 1995
760'.092—dc20 94-46522
CIP

Printed in the U.S.A.

Editor: Alan Axelrod
Art Director: Elaine Streithof
Vice President, Design: Michael J. Walsh
Production Manager: Ellen Bedell
Production Coordinator: Caroline Reaves

Note: Dimensions throughout are height x width.

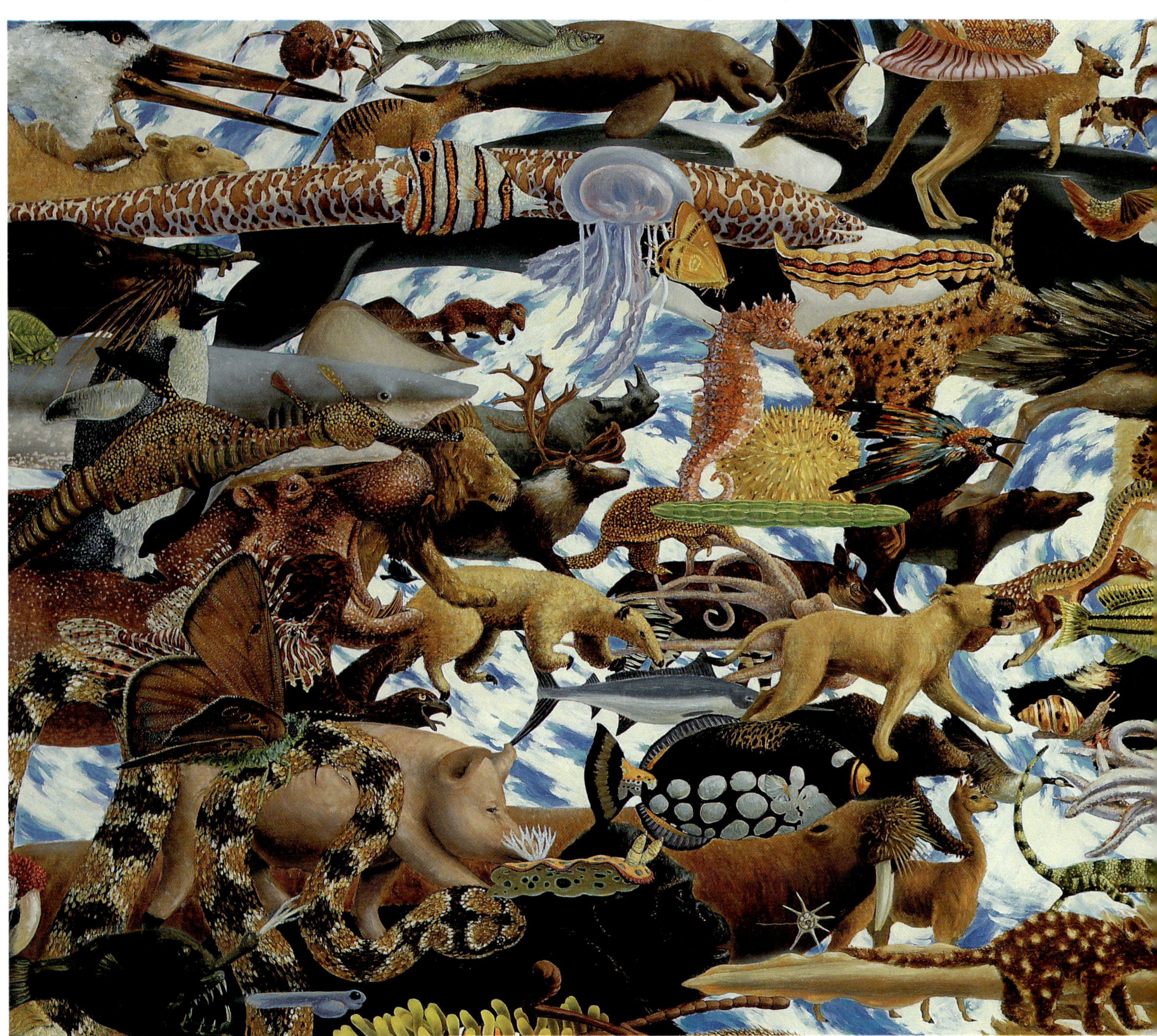

I would like to dedicate this book to my mom,

Jennie Tomao Bragg, and my dad, Charles Bragg.

SPACE RACE

1981, acrylic and oil on mylar, 36 x 72 in.

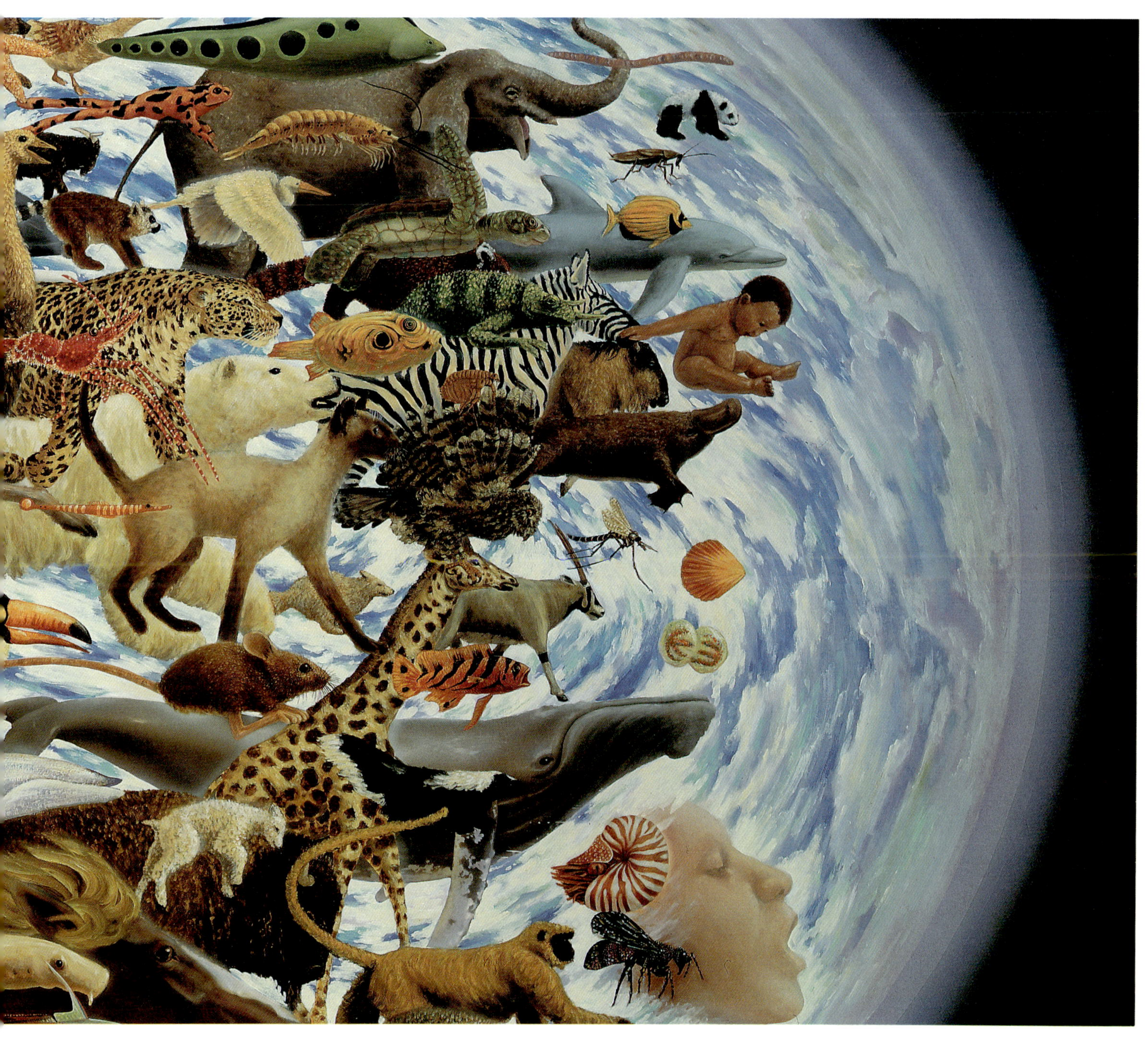

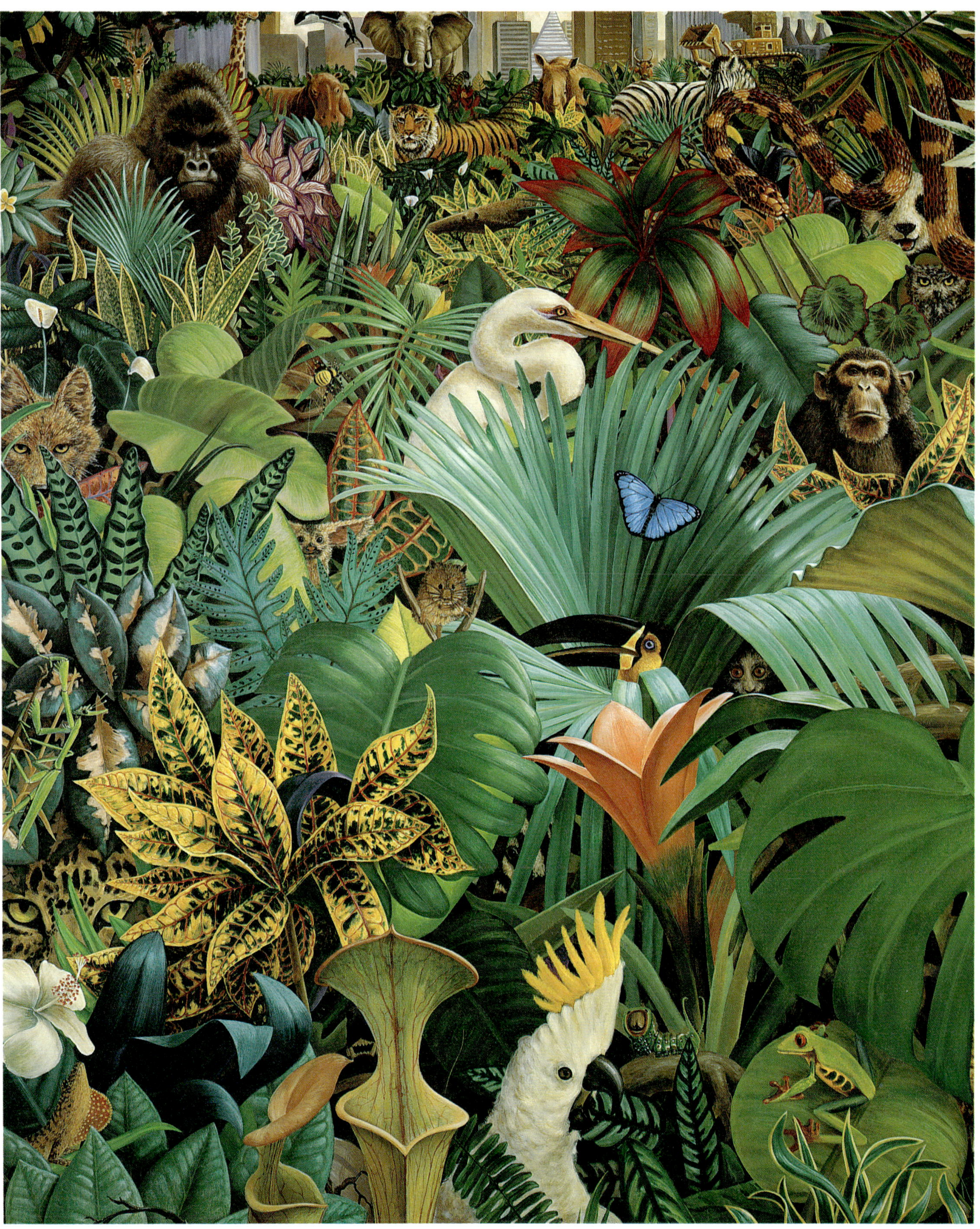

Introduction

by Geoffrey Taylor

The animalscapes of Charles Lynn Bragg are compounded of passion, personal conviction, consummate skill, and a commitment to hard work. As the natural world is increasingly overwhelmed by human "progress," speaking out in nature's defense gains greater urgency. Bragg's paintings speak of and to nature's elemental truth. It is historically important work. Humankind civilizes. Nature gets a little more squashed. Artists like Bragg are there to remind us just how fragile the balance of life is. His art is both realistic and whimsical: dead-on serious and seriously bemused. Bragg's one unwavering point: taking care of our mother ship is our vital business, no matter how much plutonium has gone under the bridge already. Be aware. Try to do something. Respect life. But don't lose your sense of humor in the process.

Bragg creates out of belief and commitment, but he knows that life requires living among the unreformed. He gets along. He talks to meat eaters. And he knows that if he can make his point with wit, he just might leave a lasting impression. His art just might make a difference.

Given the popularity of what he does, it certainly feels as if a difference is being made right here and now. Charles Lynn Bragg's environmental landscapes are showing up everywhere. They are in museums and private collections, as well as on office walls, calendars, puzzles, textbooks, and even the U.S. mail. His 1994 *Wonders of the Sea* was issued as a first-class postage stamp in an edition of 250,000,000—twice the customary Postal Service print run. For young and old all over the world, his special view of nature and its friends has become familiar, comforting, and delightful, as well as a wry admonition and warning.

Bragg's viewpoint is distinctive for its subtlety and drollness. You are often first attracted to the delicacy of some forest creature stopping by a brook, only to discover still deeper and deeper murmurs in the surrounding woods. Every rocky nook and fallen leaf reveals more life. And not just matter-of-fact life, but life with a personality, life with a heart, life that you care about. It is this life vision that has created the Charles Lynn Bragg phenomenon that began in the 1980s and is burgeoning through the '90s.

Animalscapes

Most familiar among Bragg's works are his animal landscapes. Lush, dense, and dazzlingly intricate, they are kaleidoscopic and improbable. The animal and vegetable displays are by no means random and accidental. Their look and postures always speak to a point.

In his most famous work, *City Limits*, all the usual animal animosities have been

---

City Limits

1986, acrylic on canvas, 52 x 44 in.

(opposite)

momentarily suspended. Lions and tigers and elephants are untroubled by one another's company, and the entire group is united by a singular feature: their collective gaze. Intense and unblinking, each pair of eyes looks dead-on and right at you. The gaze of the rodent is timid and delicate. That of the toucan, clear and direct. The panda looks at us, somehow wise and strangely forgiving. The leopard's glare is rich with feline wisdom, while the primates glower with the look of a silently disapproving cousin. As you contemplate them, they contemplate you right back, and you begin to understand what is going on.

"Most of the animals are staring at you," Bragg points out. "That's usually how I do it. It's a confrontation. When the animals are looking out at us, we're part of them. We connect with each other."

As the giant blandness of the city crowds in from the horizon, the animals gather to stare us down, to confront us. Don't forget about us. We're in this together.

Looking for Charles Lynn Bragg

Judging from his art, you might expect to find Charles Lynn Bragg hidden away on some island oasis, deep amid ferns and palm fronds, far from anything urban.

The truth is otherwise. You'll find Bragg's residence on a very generic, very suburban West Los Angeles street. It is an unassuming tract house in a decidedly unremarkable neighborhood. No lush flora, no animal menagerie. Except for a few colorful pots of flowers on the front stoop, the Bragg lair is quite ungreen. The house itself is brown.

You stroll around to the side and call through the slats of a wooden gate. The latch is pulled, and there you are: face to face with Mr. Bragg. He is a middle-sized, pleasantly handsome man known to all his friends by his lifelong nickname, Chick. He projects a warmth and serenity one immediately connects with many of the animal faces his imagination has brought to life. He is graceful and athletic, calm and controlled. He welcomes you warmly, and you begin the journey into understanding where all this

WONDERS OF THE SEA
U.S. Postal Stamp Collection

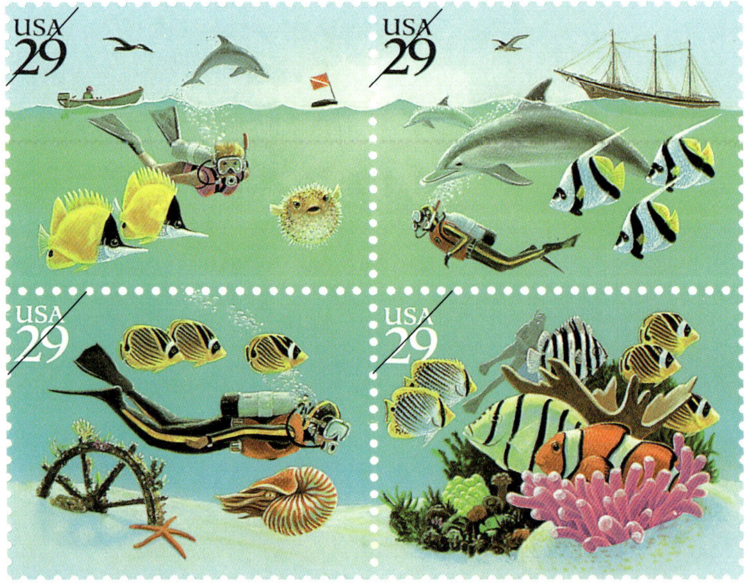

"stuff"—as he good-naturedly refers to his works and works in progress—comes from.

Nestled behind the little brown house is an equally brown and unpromising two-car garage. Beside it is a patch of dead grass ringed by a scruffy-looking cinderblock fence. Bragg unceremoniously pulls the garage door open and reveals his work space: a densely packed room chockablock with counters and cabinets and drawers and files. It accommodates only one person, and judging from the orderliness of it all, a very particular person indeed.

At the center of the space is an old wooden desk, the kind that was standard office issue thirty or forty years ago. A worn and rickety paint-speckled swivel chair is behind it, and when you sit in that chair and look out the open front of the garage, as Bragg has done for the countless hours he spends there plying his craft, it is not some inspirational vista that you behold, but another plain brown wall, with a sun-bleached back seat from an old Chevy van leaning up against it, along with a pile of forlorn-looking cement blocks, the intended purpose of which is now long forgotten.

Bragg attempts hospitality by offering you your own seat, a well-worn stationary exercise bike, whose built-in fan mechanism appears also to be the only air conditioning unit for the place. Fearing you'll be recruited to start cooling the room, you decline and remain standing. But the absent creature comforts are quickly forgotten as he starts to show you his wares. Drawer after drawer is opened, revealing photos and posters and sketches of the collected works of Charles Lynn Bragg. The volume and variety of brightly colored exotic images are overwhelming. It becomes even more astounding when you realize that most of it has been created in the brief expanse of a little over fifteen years. Out of this dimly lit little room, a seemingly endless collection of creatures and images has somehow come to life.

But where is it exactly that all these images come from?

"An idea, a word, a phrase, a joke, an experience," Bragg ticks off.

Not to mention good genes.

Getting Started

Bragg's father is Charles Bragg, a world-famous artist whose etchings and oil paintings are full of ribald characters caught in the middle of their most ludicrously human moments. His mother, Jenny Tomao, is a master of luminous oil landscapes, as notable for their serene unpeopled vistas as those of the senior Bragg are for their overpeopled ones. You see in the younger Bragg's work the synthesis of his parents'. You see his mother's aesthetic grace and his father's improbable comic drama. The setting of their son's theater may be the desert, the ocean, or the forest.

His players?

"Bambi and a bulldozer," he volunteers.

Bragg's own day-to-day participation in nature began some forty-two years ago in Detroit, Michigan. He was born prematurely, weighing only five pounds, and spent his first month on this planet in an incubator. Once he was turned loose, he more than made up for his slow start. His childhood nickname was "the Gorilla," with reference to his athletic prowess rather than to any simian qualities. In the mid 1950s, Charles and Jenny moved their son and his younger sister, Georgia (today also an accomplished artist), to the promised land of the West Coast, and California is the only place Bragg has ever thought of as home.

His first artistic medium was the crayon. His first work, a coloring book. As with many other things, the obsessive Bragg got a little carried away. Today he boasts of a still expanding collection of nearly two thousand crayons. But before long, coloring books gave way to pen and ink. At the age of ten, he would spend endless hours meticulously mimicking the line drawings of another artist. This exercise got him thinking about animals and animal anatomy. Bragg has always been fascinated by how things in nature look and how you draw them to make them look the way they do. In his studio today, early pen and ink studies stand comfortably alongside ones he did only last week.

Bragg eagerly pulls out one of his favorite books from the fifties, an educational one chock-full of gatefold dioramas depicting hypothetical scenes from the Jurassic age: brontosaurs and tyrannosaurs and pterodactyls all crammed together on some volcanic plain—a prehistoric foreshadowing of the landscapes for which Charles Lynn Bragg would become famous. He savors the irony.

The young Bragg was no bookish introvert locked in his room with paper and pen and paint and crayons. He was much too busy being a star athlete and teen heartthrob at high school in the San Fernando Valley. He was class president and voted the Person You Most Want to Be Stranded on an Island With.

It was at about this time that Bragg fell in love. The object of his affections: surfing. Twenty-seven years later, it remains his driving passion. Surf often runs him. When he's away from it for too long, he loses something elemental to his nature. Without the surf, art and creativity seem irrelevant and unavailable to him. "I get depressed if there's a swell and I can't go."

Bragg's art is clearly linked to the surfer in him. He is the archetypal surf dude, bobbing tiny and solitary in the deep water, immersing himself in the swells, riding the crests, mastering the rolls for a brief moment only to regroup once again and diligently paddle back to sea, awaiting the next opportunity. This is much the same way in which he approaches his art. He has always been a searcher. He has a profound need to be in tune with the world around him. "It's not really that I'm looking for subject matter. I'm just looking for peace of mind," he says. After high school, searching for such peace meant following the ocean swells. Traveling and surfing kept him blissfully unfocused, even while he stopped briefly to get some formal art training at Cal Arts.

Getting Started with Art

The professional artist part of Bragg's story evolved innocently enough. His parents shared a workspace in a little rented house in Encino. They used the bedrooms as their studios, and Bragg printed his dad's etchings in the kitchen and dried them in the living room. He would surf during the day, work out at the local gym, and earn money printing etchings whenever he needed the income. He had it made: just enough money to pay the rent and get gas for his van.

Inevitably, as he printed his father's etchings, Bragg started to get ideas about things he could make himself. His first attempt was called *A Boy with Marbles*. His dad taught him some basic etching techniques, such as how to manipulate the plate to get the desired effect.

Did his father have any other advice to offer?

"Work, work, work," the younger Bragg replies dryly.

Within a short time, he was selling enough of his own prints to motivate him to do more. He knew he was onto something.

"All of a sudden I had a business."

At the time, this was not so clearly the beginning of a career as the beginning of a beginning. His success with the etchings led him to set up his own rudimentary studio in the back bedroom of a modest apartment right next to the beach in Santa Monica. The next ten years of work were the real learning curve, during which Bragg's art and, perhaps more importantly, his technique were honed. He produced abstracts, pencil drawings, paintings, and prints, mastering different methods, different mediums, different themes. His overhead was minimal. Artistically, he did whatever he felt like doing. And: "I learned an awful lot."

Commissions provided him with his bread and butter. Or his agent would tell him that he could really use some cats, and Bragg would produce some cats—great, beautiful cats, which also sold well and brought a bit more recognition (not to mention a bit more money). Suddenly—it seemed—Bragg found himself in the middle of a career he had never anticipated.

Of course, whenever he hit on a commercial success—a noble stallion or an august leopard—he was inevitably tempted to do more like it. Animal studies were especially accessible and popular. Demand led to better and better commissions. But it was never a completely easy fit. He would inevitably drift back into esoterica, into art that was definitely not warm and fuzzy, stubbornly resisting enslavement to the marketplace. He did, however, decide one thing for certain along the way. He *would* be an artist. He'd been around paints and brushes his whole life without really thinking of them as the tools of his trade. Making art was just something he did, something his whole family did. Suddenly, he realized that art was not just what he did. It was what he wanted to do.

And through it all, his technique was becoming razor sharp. The only question was

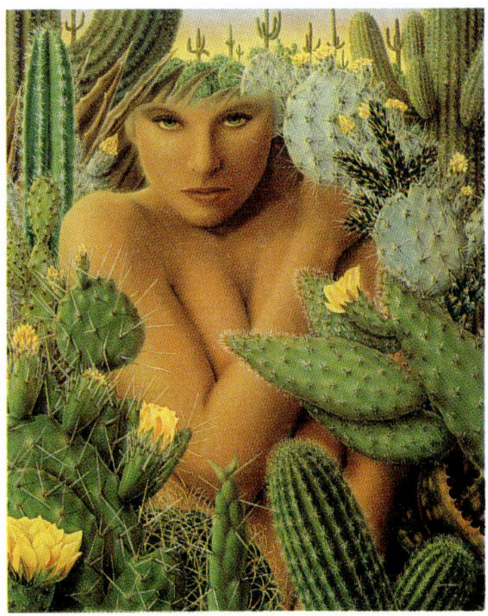

DESERT EVE

1986, acrylic on canvas, 36 x 30 in.

Bull's-eye Zebra

1994, pen and ink 10 x 11 in.

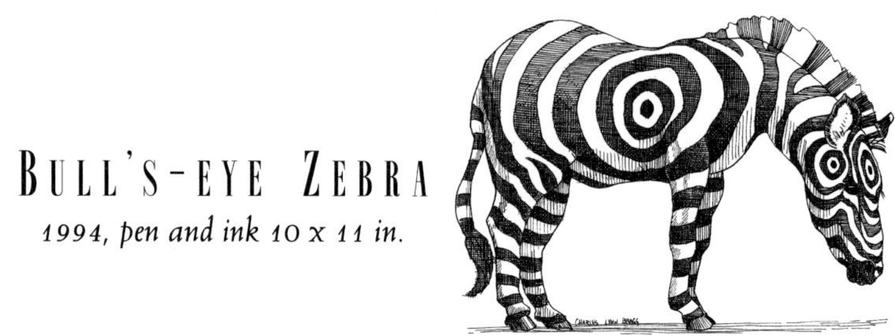

just how to make use of it. Fill the commissions and feed the marketplace? Or go his own way—and maybe starve in the process?

Ironically, it was during one of his going-his-own-way moods that Bragg produced *City Limits* (1987), the single most important work of his career so far. He had decided to paint another surrealistic woman-in-nature piece, along the lines of *Desert Eve* (1986), except this time she would be nested among jungle life. He painted her over and over, moved her, dressed her and undressed her. Nothing worked. So he painted her out completely and replaced her with a jungle menagerie. The rest is history.

City Limits, produced as a hugely popular poster lithograph edition, was Bragg's first monster success. He had found access to the masses. And he liked it.

Getting Back to the Garden

After *City Limits*, Bragg decided that he would travel around the world to experience habitats and environments firsthand, to seek out real-life adventures and paint them. He would become an adventurer-artist. After surfing, his greatest passion became nature and research trips: journeys to exotic locales, where he could hang out with indigenous wildlife, far from the distractions of telephones, galleries, and agents. Bragg has been high up into the California Sierras, across the Mexican Baja and Anza Borrego deserts, deep into the Costa Rican jungle, among the underwater coral reefs of Bali, and into the Australian Outback. He schedules new adventures all the time in order to stock his visual memory, on which he calls to reproduce the tiniest details: the patina of a mushroom's flesh, the crinkle of a drying leaf—all the particulars of living and dying, which are the true processes of any natural environment.

Bragg says he just doesn't feel completely honest if he hasn't experienced for himself at least part of what he's painting. When people admire *African Watering Hole* and ask him if he's been to Africa, he has to admit he hasn't. "I feel like I've let them down."

Nowadays, he rarely has to apologize to his fans. Before he begins work on one of his large animal landscapes, his first order of business is to plan the trip and look through his drawers which are crammed with photographs from past adventures. Asked about a specific element in a landscape, he can tell you just how a certain howler monkey swung above him, across the canopy of the Costa Rican rain forest, just like the one in a painting.

The key to understanding Charles Lynn Bragg is to know that the compulsive disciplined artist guy is trapped inside a serendipitous surfer guy. His constant search for good, uncrowded waves is a driving force that often overpowers his creative needs. If you were to come across Bragg while he's hanging out with his surf buddies, you would think him just another wet-suited dude waiting for a great wave. And so, it is no accident that some of the "nature" places he returns to over and over again also happen to offer some of the finest surfing on the planet. One remote beach in Java takes two days of travel to reach, but once there, immersion in sea and jungle is total. "I don't need to go looking for the waves or the jungle. I'm in it."

Bragg fantasizes about the day when he will permanently adopt the island life: Gauguin conditions . . . with satellite access to the marketplace. "But I'm sure I'd still travel all over the place. The world is just too interesting not to go after."

For the present, his days in Los Angeles begin with putting the coffee on and arranging his studio in preparation for the day's work. As far as surfing goes, that mile and a half separating him from the Pacific may as well be five hundred. For the artist, it's probably just as well that his little studio looks out on barren walls rather than the ocean blue.

But be it ocean or earth, at times he still misses nature. "Sometimes I just take my shoes off and go stand in the dirt in my yard."

In the Company of Giants

Bragg's bread-and-butter works are his ever-popular animalscapes, which inevitably command his primary focus. He has visited—thematically and physically—jungles and deserts and coral reefs, gathering the stuff of a Charles Lynn Bragg vista. We watch him at work on a large canvas, *In the Company of Giants* (1993). Partially finished skunks await their stripes, a squirrel his lips. Nearby, on walls and countertops, other projects crowd in, clamoring for attention. Etching plates of Native Americans, T-shirts with silkscreened hippos, half-finished human torsos and lithesome female figures dangle from nails. All patiently await the artist's rediscovery. Copies of magazines like *Ocean Realm*, *Wildlife Art News*, and *Earthwatch* are neatly filed. Art books and nature books fill many shelves. Bragg's Things to Do list is prominently posted. He tells you repeatedly that he feels the need to regroup and rethink things constantly, lest he forget why he started all this in the first place.

In the Company of Giants hangs partially complete on the studio wall. The subject matter was a logical choice for Bragg. It was found, literally speaking, in his own backyard of California, and, maybe better still, it is an especially controversial subject right now, as forests are threatened with extinction. Perfect fuel for Bragg's creativity. Work on the painting had begun months earlier with a trip to the old growth redwood forests of Northern California. After setting up camp, Bragg spent his daylight hours hiking among the enormous stands of giant sequoias, all the time taking photographs, writing notes, and making sketches. He would sit silently for hours and simply watch the daily life of the places. Sometimes that meant nothing more elaborate than the occasional butterfly or sparrow gliding by. Sometimes it meant bigger quarry. But all of this waiting and watching is essential to capturing the spirit of the place. Bragg will tell you that watching nature requires as much intense concentration as getting the images onto canvas.

Now, back in his studio, Bragg has placed many of these creatures among his own redwood stand. "It's like a family portrait: who's left in 1993," Bragg muses, as he conducts a brief tour of the ensemble he is gathering. He shows you photographs of deer and chipmunks and brown bear and skunks. A mountain lion and several eagles have been imported from other forays into other remote ecosystems. "And this scrub jay and salamander are from my backyard."

That same noisy scrub jay is a frequent visitor to Bragg's studio. He and his mate come calling every morning for their daily ration of peanuts and, one suspects, just to see their old buddy, the artist. Personal familiarity with his subjects inspires Bragg more than anything else. He has always connected with animals. When he says that they talk to him and he talks back to them, he means it. The silent, watchful eyes of his creations speak to the animal in all of us. It is hard not to be charmed by it all.

"People respond to the animals I do. They don't respond to the trees I do. They respond to the character that they find in my animals. I try and make them individuals. A deer is not a deer is not a deer is not a deer. It is alive. They are alive. They all have their own personalities. Some of them are ornery, and some of them are soft and nice. They're as unique as humans are."

Doing the Work

As you watch the artist apply color and shape to the triptych, it is clear that his hands-on research is really only the preamble to the journey. By the time he is ready to

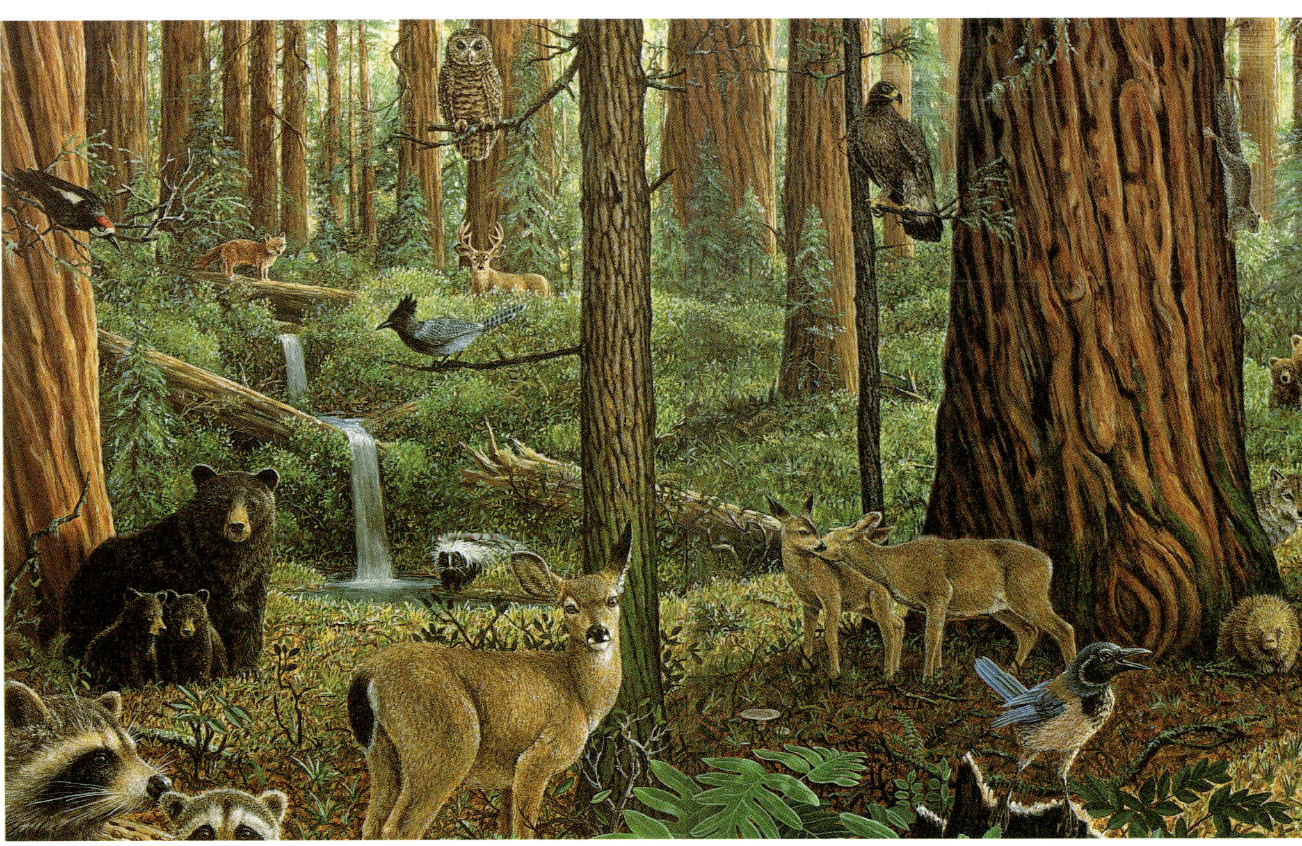

embark, his entire studio is a patchwork quilt of photographs and sketches and open books. To compensate for the nature he wasn't able to see personally, Bragg studies tapes from his extensive library of nature footage or uses his computer/video hookup to grab individual frames and examine a talon or curving tail more closely. He does slow-motion studies of the mechanics of animal movement. He blows up the detail of a fur pattern to better understand its subtle variations. Only when he becomes thoroughly saturated with his subject does he finally begin to work.

The first sketches lead quickly to endless revisions and alterations. "Everything changes," he offers casually. The first issue is that of light and perspective. Then the horizon line. Then the general placement of dominant elements.

Once he defines the background, he starts deep in the painting and slowly moves forward with more and more detail. Basic colors in the sky, then the elemental contrasts: placement of light and dark; texture to trees, fur, and rock; and then, finally, color. As a rule, he does not concern himself about specific color—other than its being warm or cool—until the final stages of the painting, at which time he will saturate and intensify the colors in order to bring the painting to life. Bragg uses the same basic palette for deep sea as for arid desert. He points out that nature uses the same palette for just about everything.

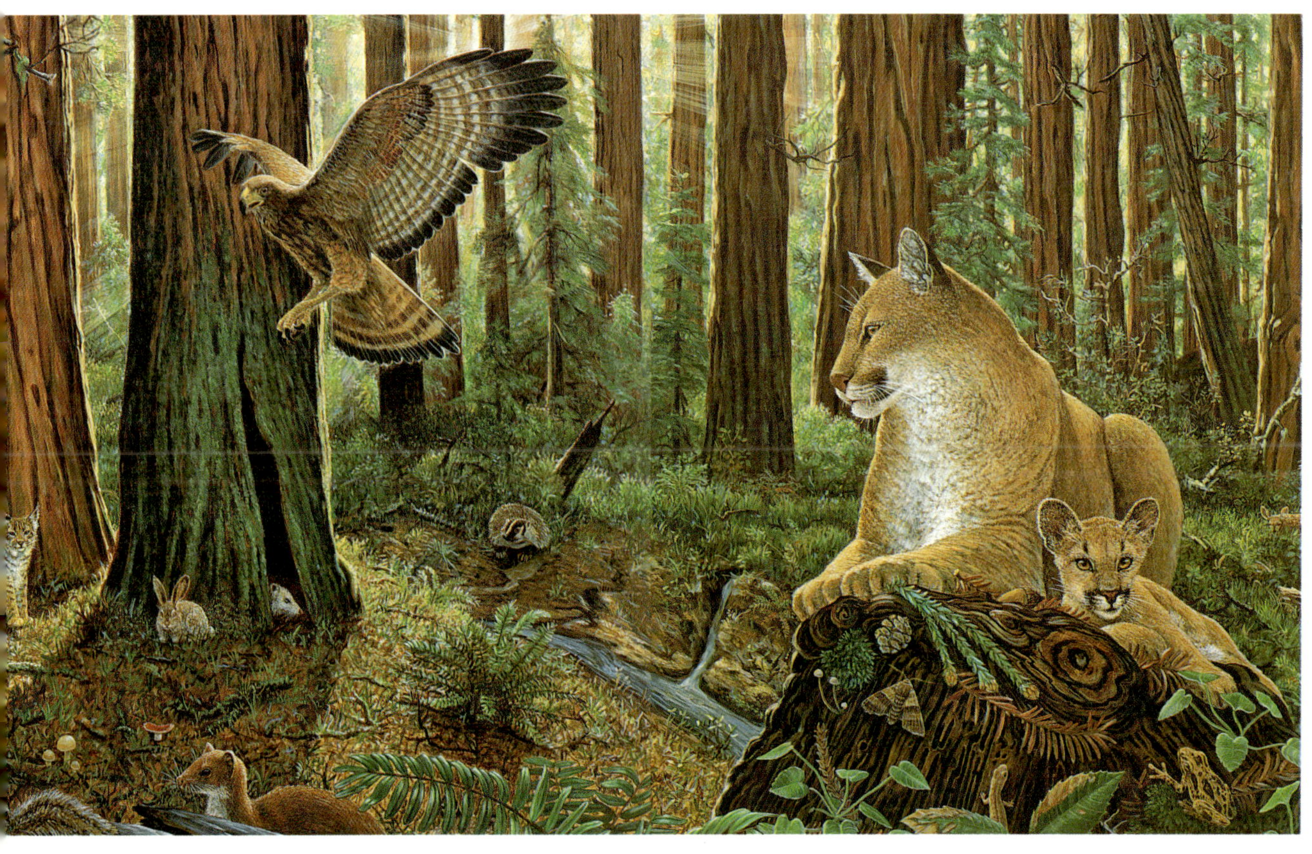

IN THE COMPANY OF GIANTS

Triptych, 1993, acrylic on canvas, 16 x 48 in. (each panel)

Mirror, Mirror

1994, pen and ink, 10 x 13 in.

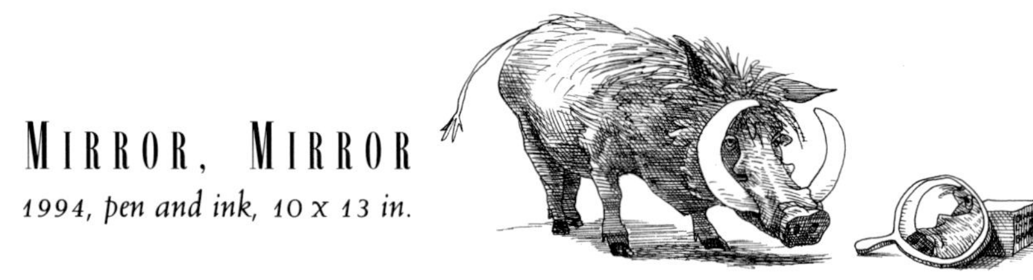

"The first part is always fun," he volunteers, but the last two-thirds of a painting requires total focus and discipline. Generalized concept, composition, and placement give way to minute bits of fur and leaf veins and eye twinkles.

Radical behavior is more the rule for Bragg than the exception. "I'll start adding elements and then, after a while, what usually happens is the animal I started with, that I started basing everything else in the painting on, doesn't fit anymore."

So Charles Lynn Bragg paints it out.

He creates, destroys, and re-creates over and over in order to make his improbable visions seem not only probable, but inevitable. He does not simply try for aesthetic harmony, but strives for naturalistic truth. The successful landscape must appear seamless. The more hours he puts into it, the less the seams will show.

The process can take six months or more for a single painting.

Awareness of this process gives fresh insight into the journey that has brought *In the Company of Giants* to its present stage. The central elements of the painting are the trees and the deer. The horizon kept moving, and the trees were repeatedly shifted and resized. The river suddenly appeared. The waterfall had to be lowered. The light source moved from one side to the other.

As Bragg talks about the changes he made to *In the Company of Giants*, you try to envision the other horizon, the animals that have come and gone, what the missing deer and skunk must have looked like, what the green failed to do that the blue does now. But, try as you might, the painting seems so right as what it has become that you don't really have any need to imagine the painting that no longer is.

The CLB Touch

When we return a few weeks later, we find the artist massaging the triptych of redwood rogues into final shape. At first glance, it is difficult to articulate the metamorphosis. Something is profoundly different, but what is it? And then you notice an extraordinary thing. It is no longer just you and Bragg standing in the studio. You have been joined by the bear and deer and jay and their pals as they peer out from their balcony position on the wall next to his desk. The studio wall has a new window, not opening onto a plain brown wall, but looking out over a little sliver of sylvan paradise. You would swear you feel cool breezes, smell the redwood, and hear the chipmunks chuckle.

This effect is an elemental part of Charles Lynn Bragg's art. It is the magical touch that marks all of his works. What he does is not finished until he imbues the work with his special animating touch. It's what sets his landscapes and animal studies apart from simple nature paintings. "A touch of Disney with a surreal twist," he calls it. On this particular Wednesday, you can see that *In the Company of Giants* has indeed undergone that magical CLB transformation.

He isn't trying for pure realism. He wants things to skew to the fantasy side. "A fox doesn't stand next to a chicken, unless the chicken is dead."

When is a painting done? How does Bragg know that the raccoon will be no better off with one more whisker? "I start running out of things I think I should do to it." When he takes the work to the laboratory to be photographed, it is as complete as it will ever be. This is the way it will be published.

So is *In the Company of Giants* really done? Bragg admits he could spend another month on it, easy. To what end? The answer is simple: "Perfection."

Then he continues: "I can never get perfection. Only nature can do that."

Bragg's Elephant

Bragg compares success to an elephant. It's something he's always wanted.

"All you think about is getting the elephant. That's all you want."

And once he got the elephant?

"You find out you've got to feed it. And that is a full-time job. Before I had the elephant to feed, my life was much simpler."

Bragg has ended up with a much larger elephant than he ever imagined. Managing a successful career has been a lot more like riding a tsunami than a righteous curl. "It sounds like I'm always in a jungle or on a hike somewhere." But since he got the elephant, he must spend a lot more time behind that little wooden desk in his studio. He laments sometimes that the career has taken on a life of its own. He works long and hard just to be able to get back to the same beach he used to go to whenever he wanted some sand and surf.

When his agent demands "more kittens . . . more kittens," Charles Lynn Bragg bristles. "I don't make french fries. I'm not a production guy." But he never apologizes for being a populist. He's a popular artist whose populism has a point: "I do know that I want to focus on this subject matter right now. Animals and environmental concerns are global issues for the nineties, and they're real issues in my life. Environmental statements do make a difference to me. I want to make them because we don't have much time to make them before we're gone. We can make a difference, so that we will have a world worth living in fifty years from now. Not just a dust bowl."

In spite of some occasional grumbling, Bragg is quite fond of his elephant. He is especially pleased that his acceptance coincides with the renewed global interest in environmentalism. Animal rights and ecology groups worldwide are using Bragg's paintings to remind people how delicate a vessel our little blue planet is. And how precious her cargo.

The tension between commerce and art will always be a part of his craft and career. Work, work, work. New challenges and new complications.

"As an artist, you're supposed to get frustrated with things. Otherwise, what's the point and where's the beauty?"

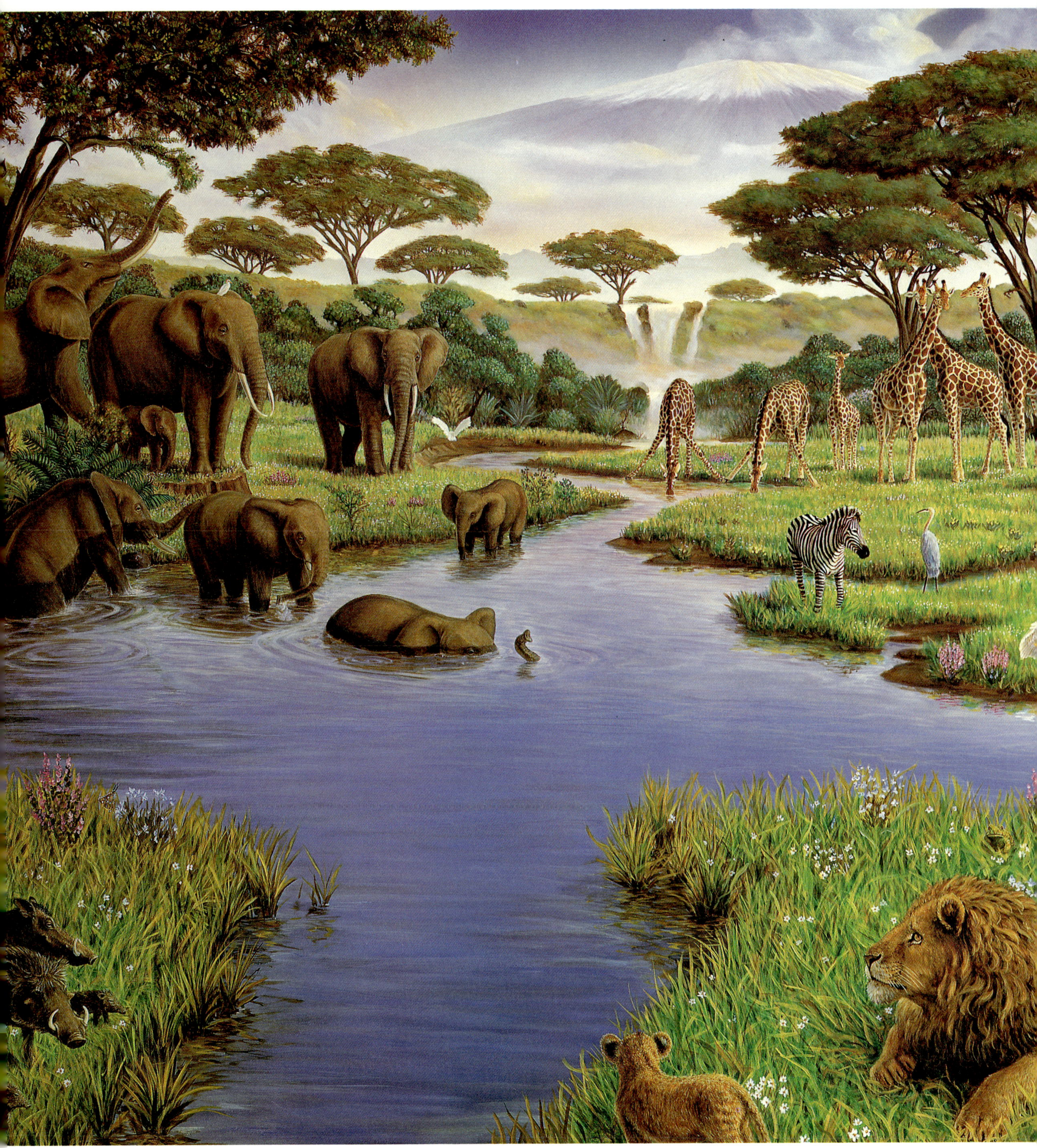

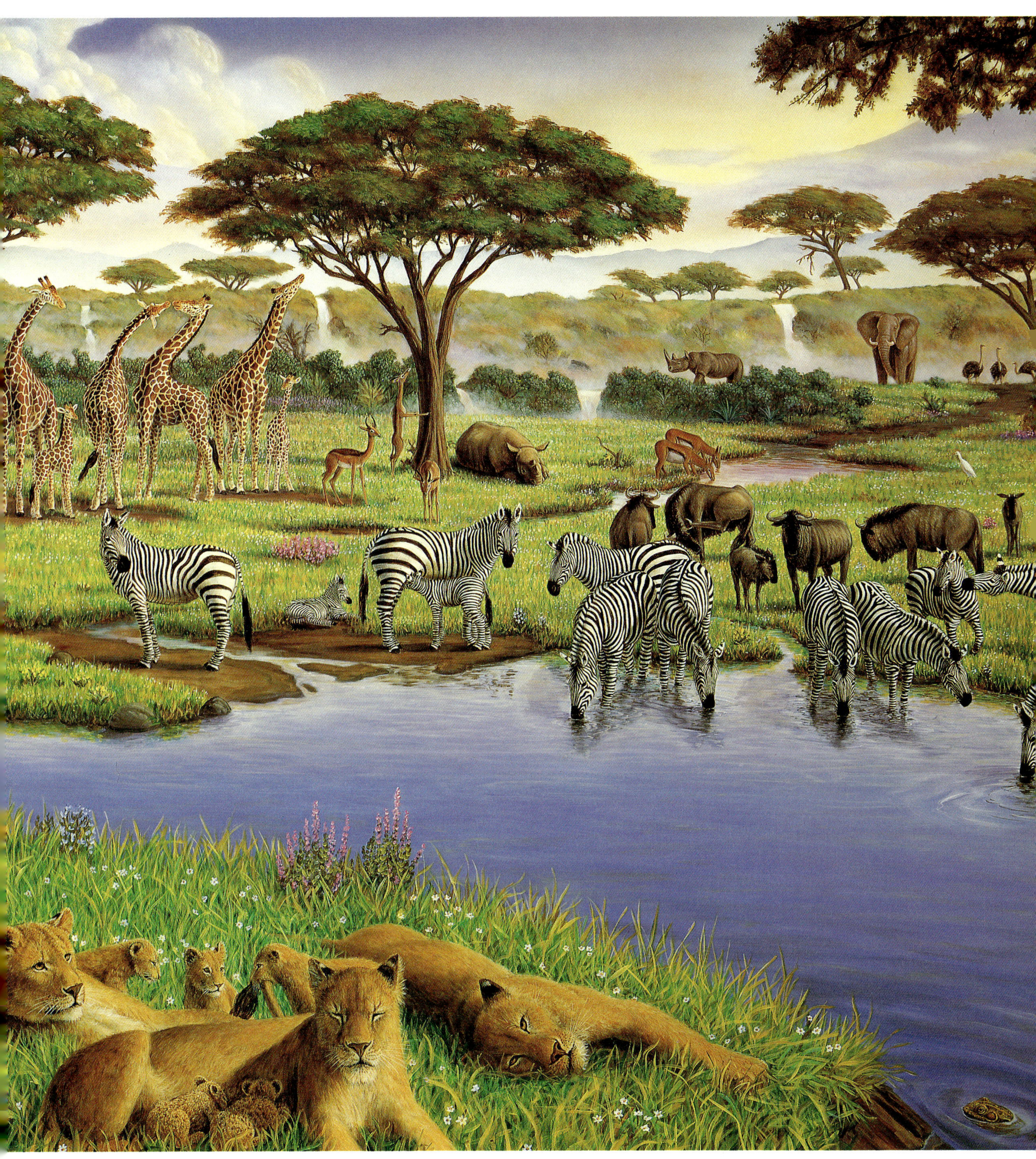

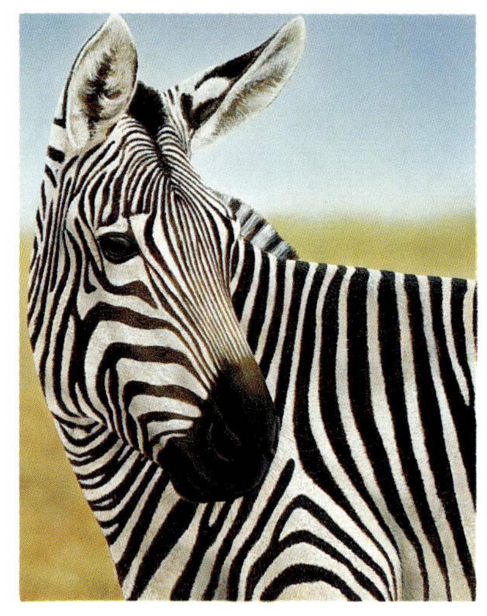

Zebra

1990, acrylic on canvas, 20 x 16 in.

Baby Indian Elephant

1993, acrylic and oil on board, 12 x 10 in.

He was my first trip back into oil paints after eight years of working only in acrylics. I mixed all my colors in advance. I wanted to do something small. I was doing it to experiment with oils, and I wanted to simplify any problems I might have. I projected the slide of an elephant on a board, and I traced the outline of the elephant, then painted him in. I really liked how I was able to get the darks and lights. He's so cute and shy and vulnerable. How does that happen? I don't know.

African Watering Hole

1989, acrylic and oil on canvas, 48 x 96 in.

(Previous spread)

The painting is 4 by 8 feet, and it's a very happy group of animals. Even the warthogs look good. Of course, you can't see the pile of zebra bones in front of the lions. But that explains why they're so sedate.

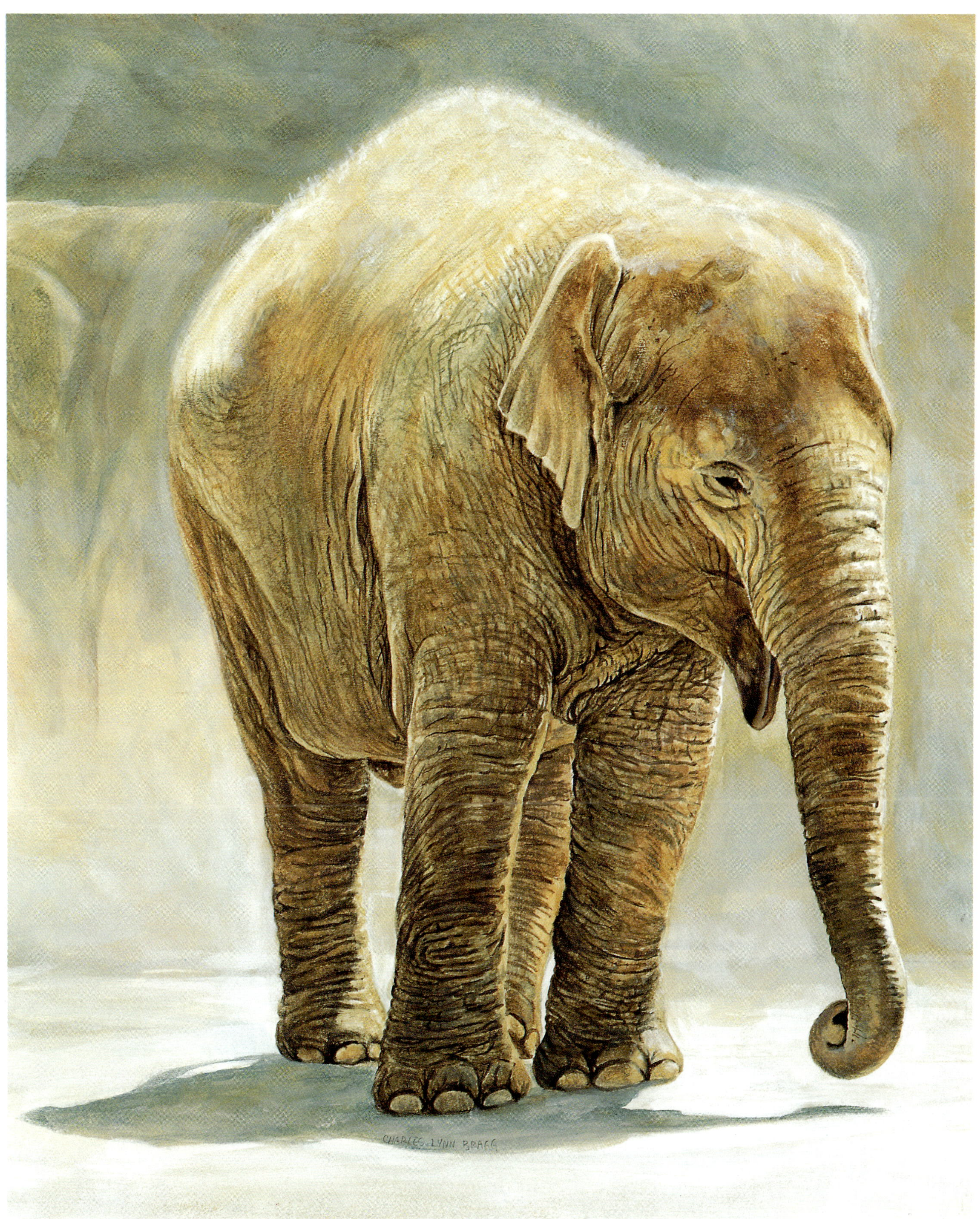
CHARLES LYNN BRAGG

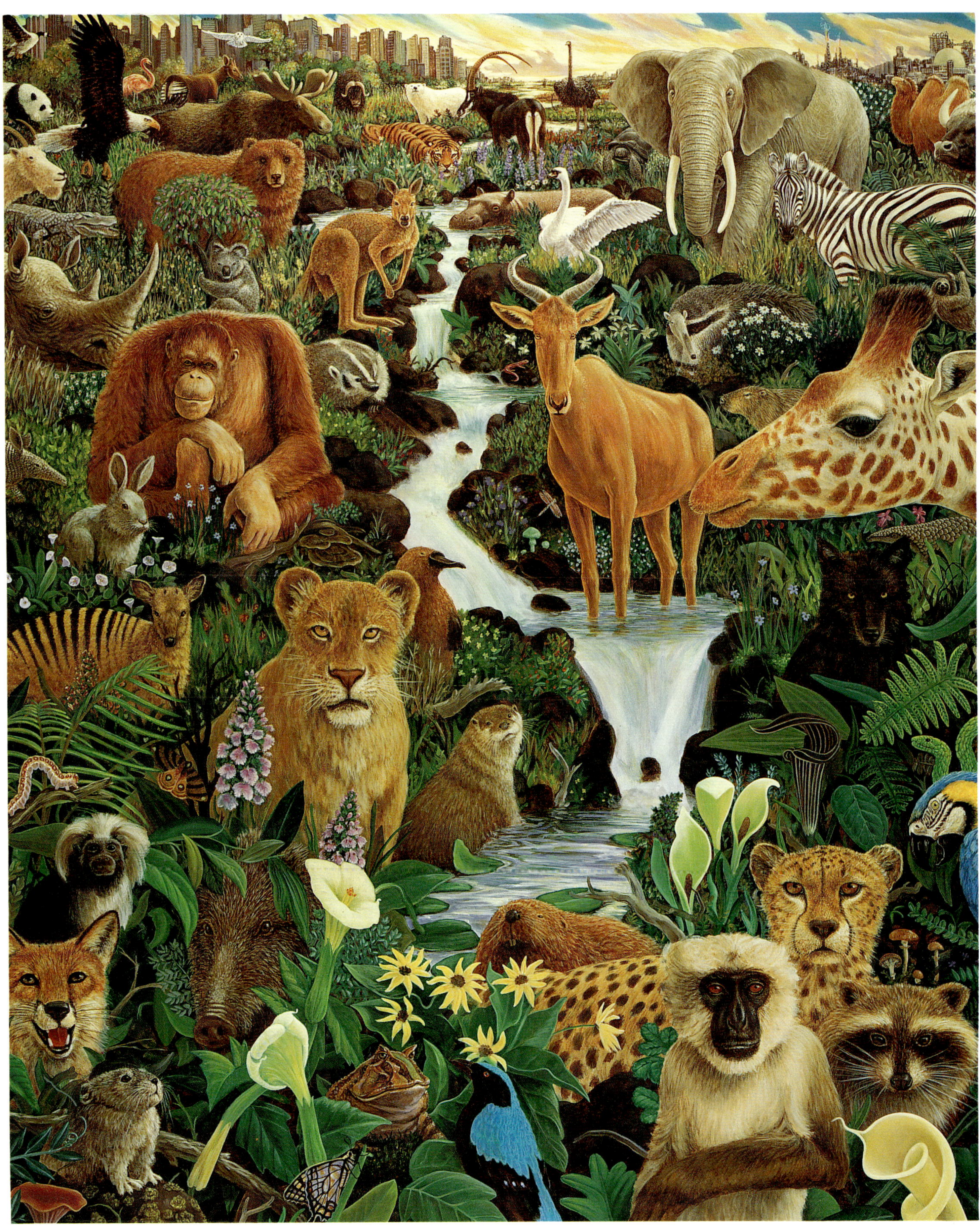

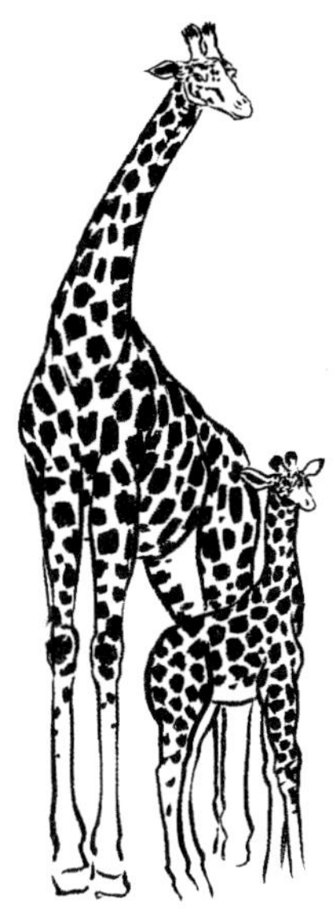

Mother and Baby Giraffes

1994, ink on paper, 14 x 11 in.

Animal Magnetism

1989, acrylic on canvas, 48 x 40 in.

This was a commission from Gil Michaels, the publisher of *Animal's Voice Magazine*. He wanted to get the *City Limits* painting, but it was already sold, so he commissioned this one. I recast it with completely different animals. Some of the characters here I really like: the orangutan, the giraffe. Someone once asked me how I made the giraffe smile. It's even odder when you think about how they eat. They have nineteen-inch black tongues, which pluck the leaves off incredibly thorny acacia trees.

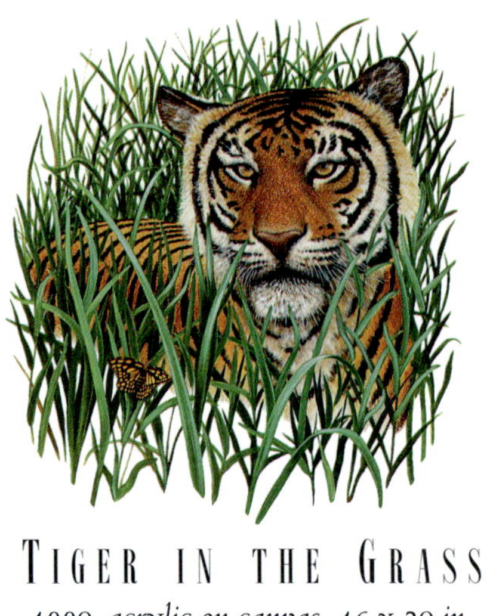

Tiger in the Grass

1990, acrylic on canvas, 16 x 20 in.

Twilight of the Tiger

1987, acrylic on canvas, 48 x 60 in.

This one is 4 by 6 feet: almost life size. It was something I wanted to do. I played around on my computer, putting together different images and ideas, and ended up putting him together with a freeway. I thought, "Here we are, losing the tiger, but what are we gaining?" Off ramps, railroad tracks, crashed cars along the road.

Some trade-off.

I think that tiger is down in Laguna Beach now . . . just roaming around.

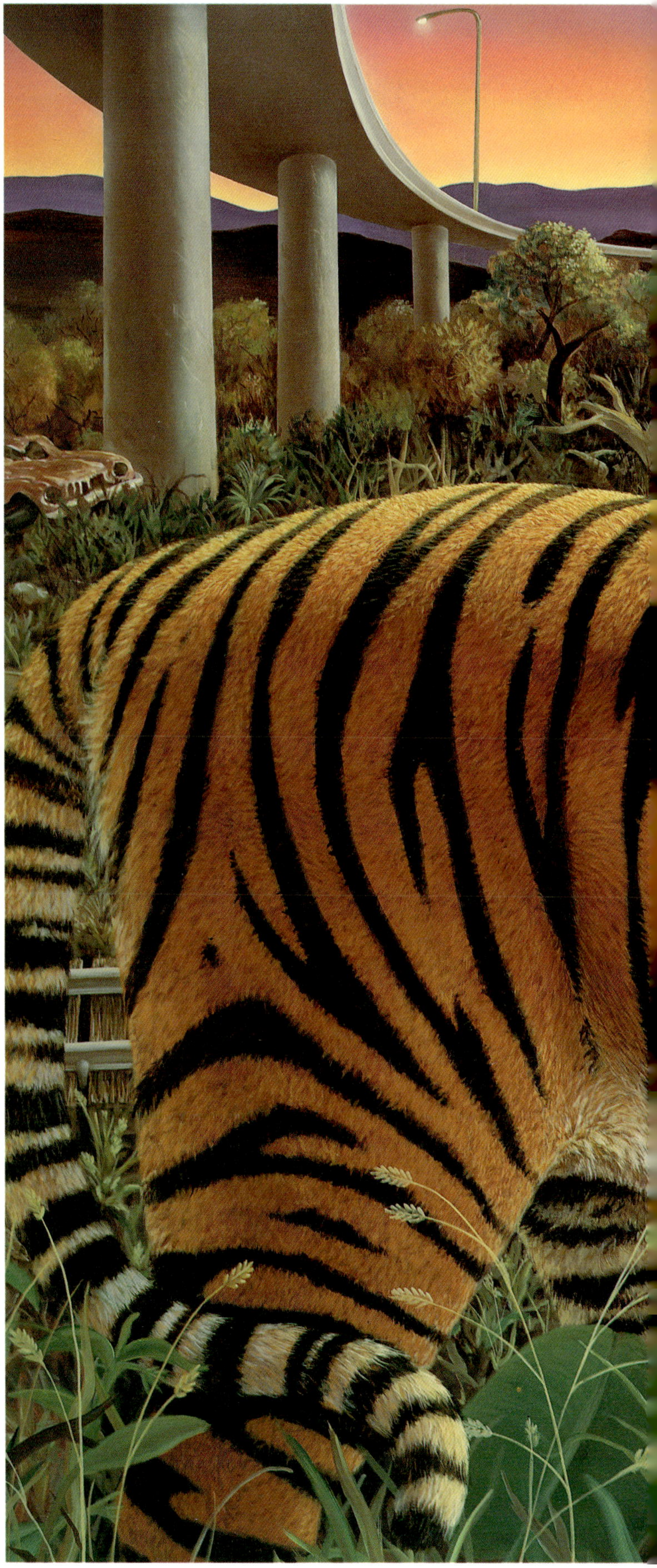

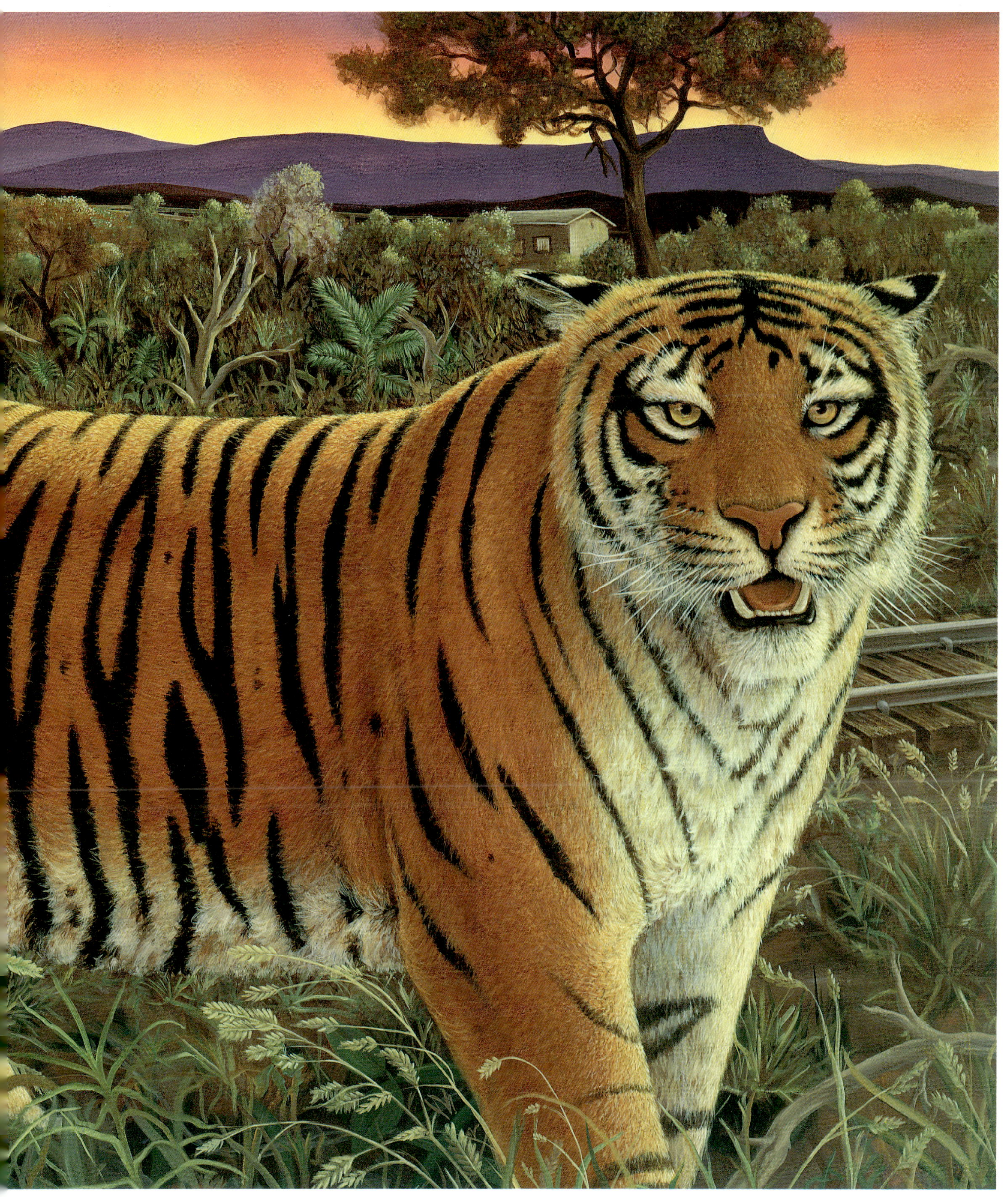

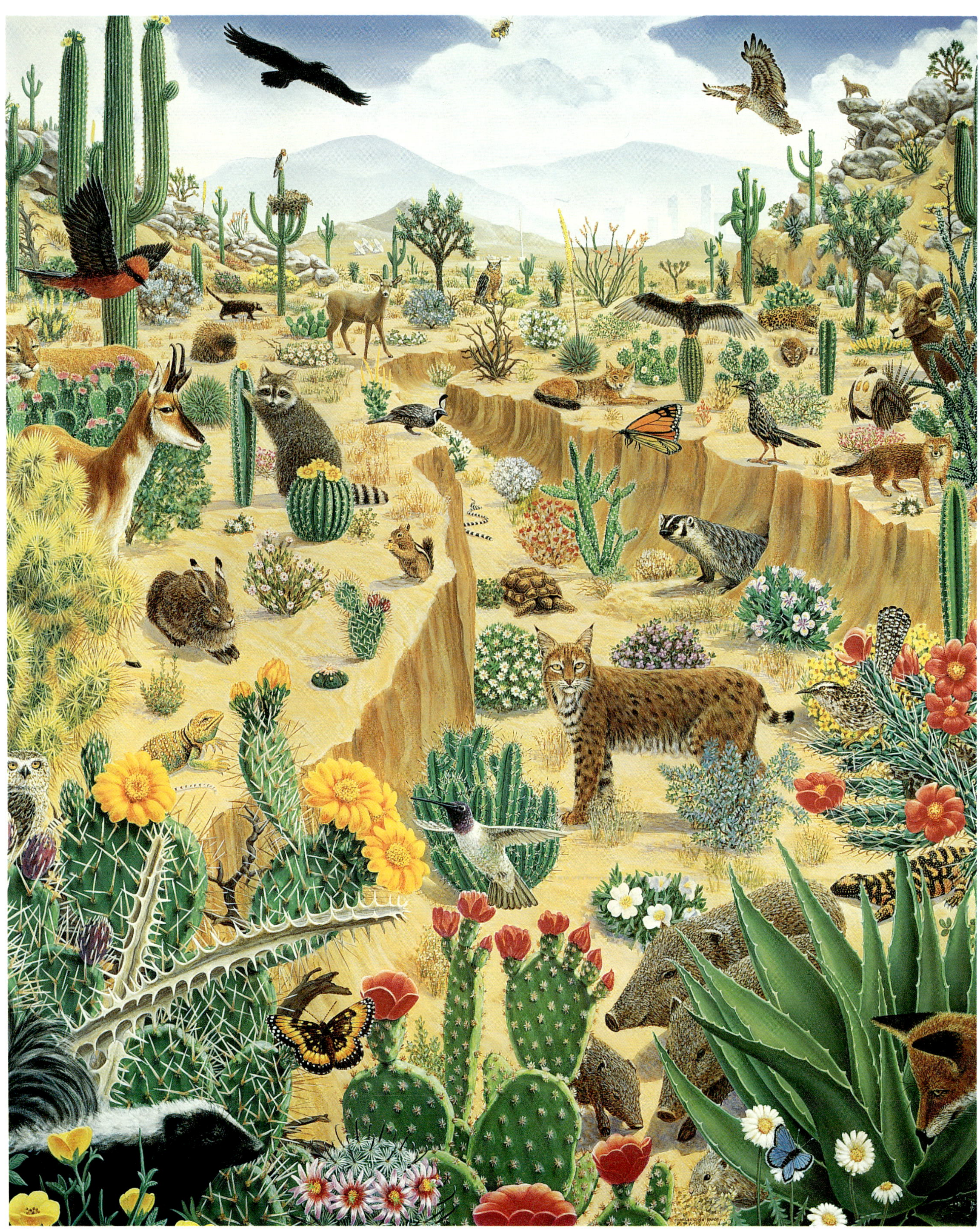

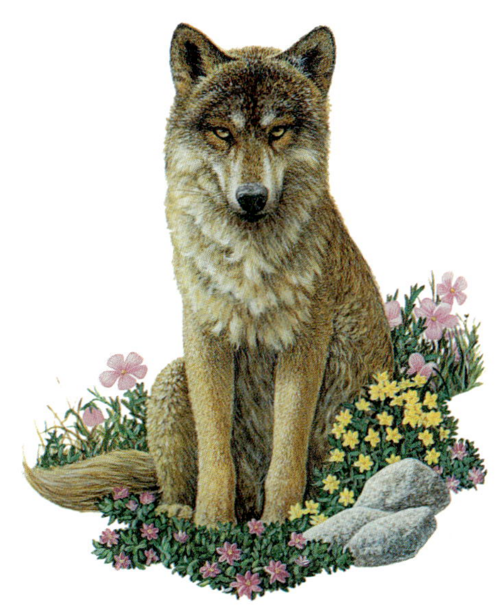

Wolf

1990, acrylic on canvas, 20 x 16 in.

Last Oasis

1989, acrylic on canvas, 48 x 40 in.

It's often theme and variation, and *Last Oasis* is one of the variations. I really like this one. There's a city—way, way in the background. I was thinking of Las Vegas, with radar dishes and atomic testing.

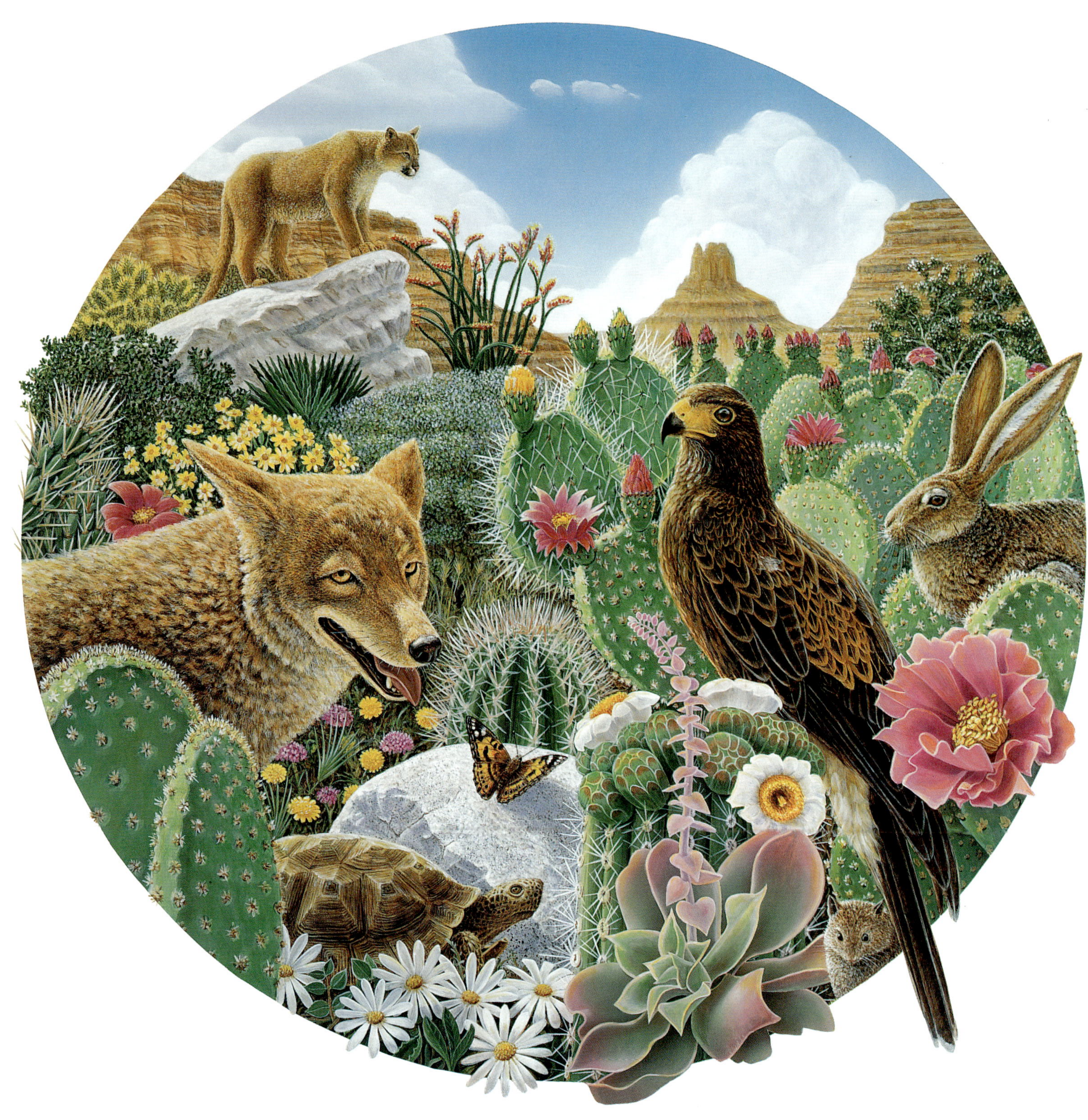

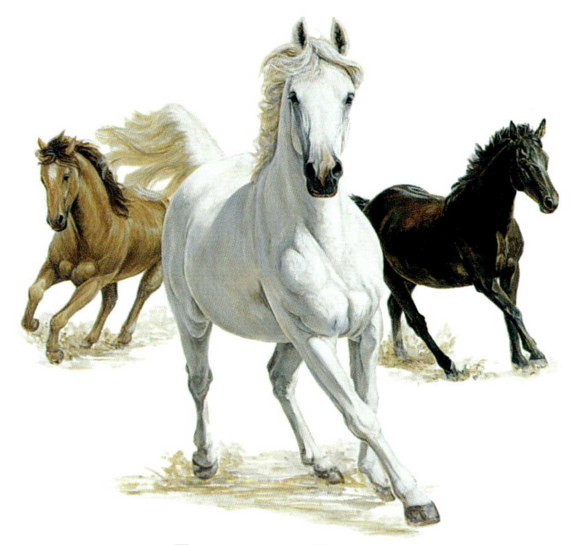

Three Horses

1991, acrylic on canvas, 16 x 20 in.

Desert Roundup

1992, acrylic on canvas, D: 21 in.

This is the southern California desert. I went to the Anza Borrego Desert in the spring, the season when the flowers bloom. I camped out, hiked, and meditated for a couple of days. The hawk and coyote I observed at a game reserve, and the cougar was at Shambala, Tippi Hedren's wild animal ranch. All the plants were from Anza Borrego.

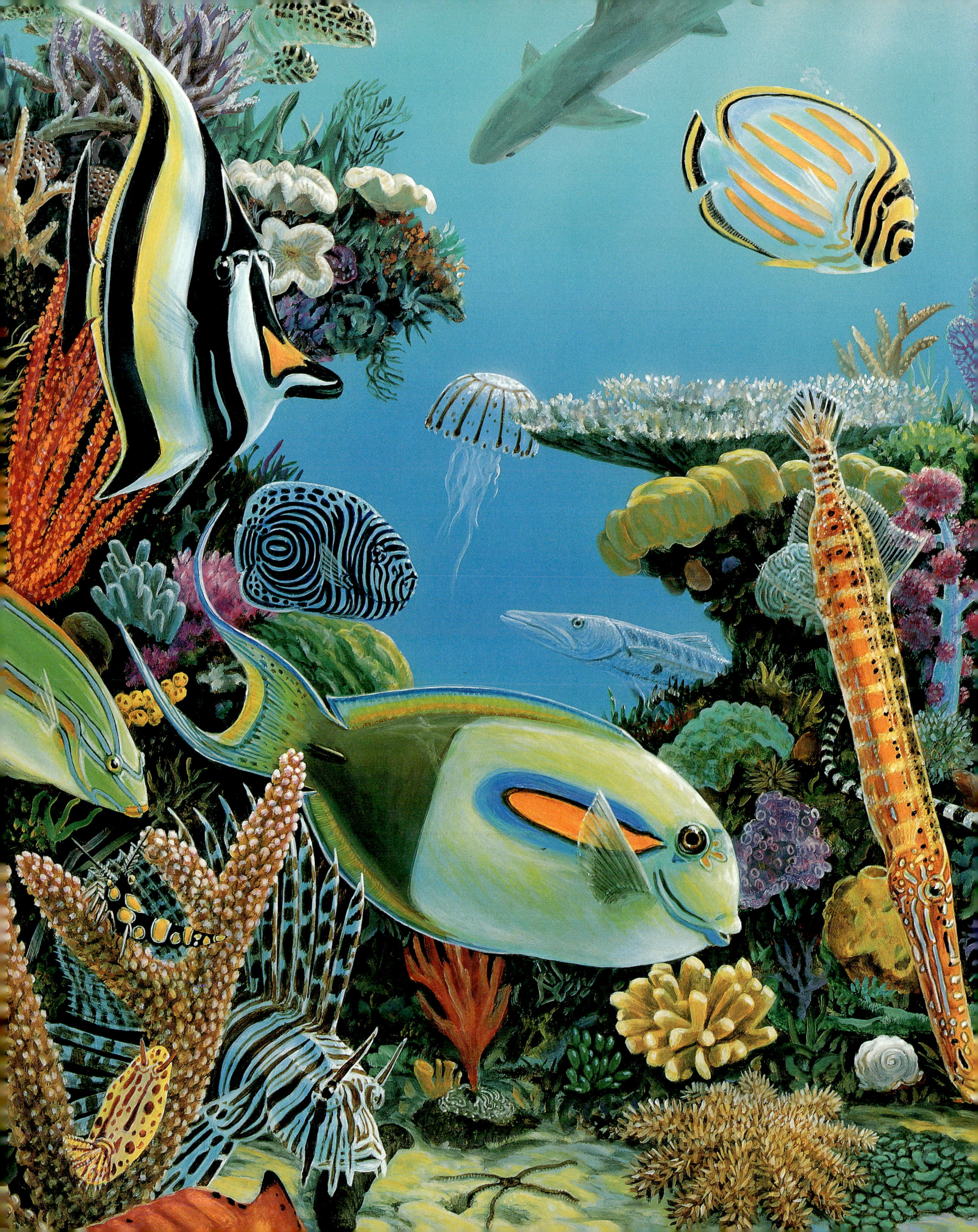

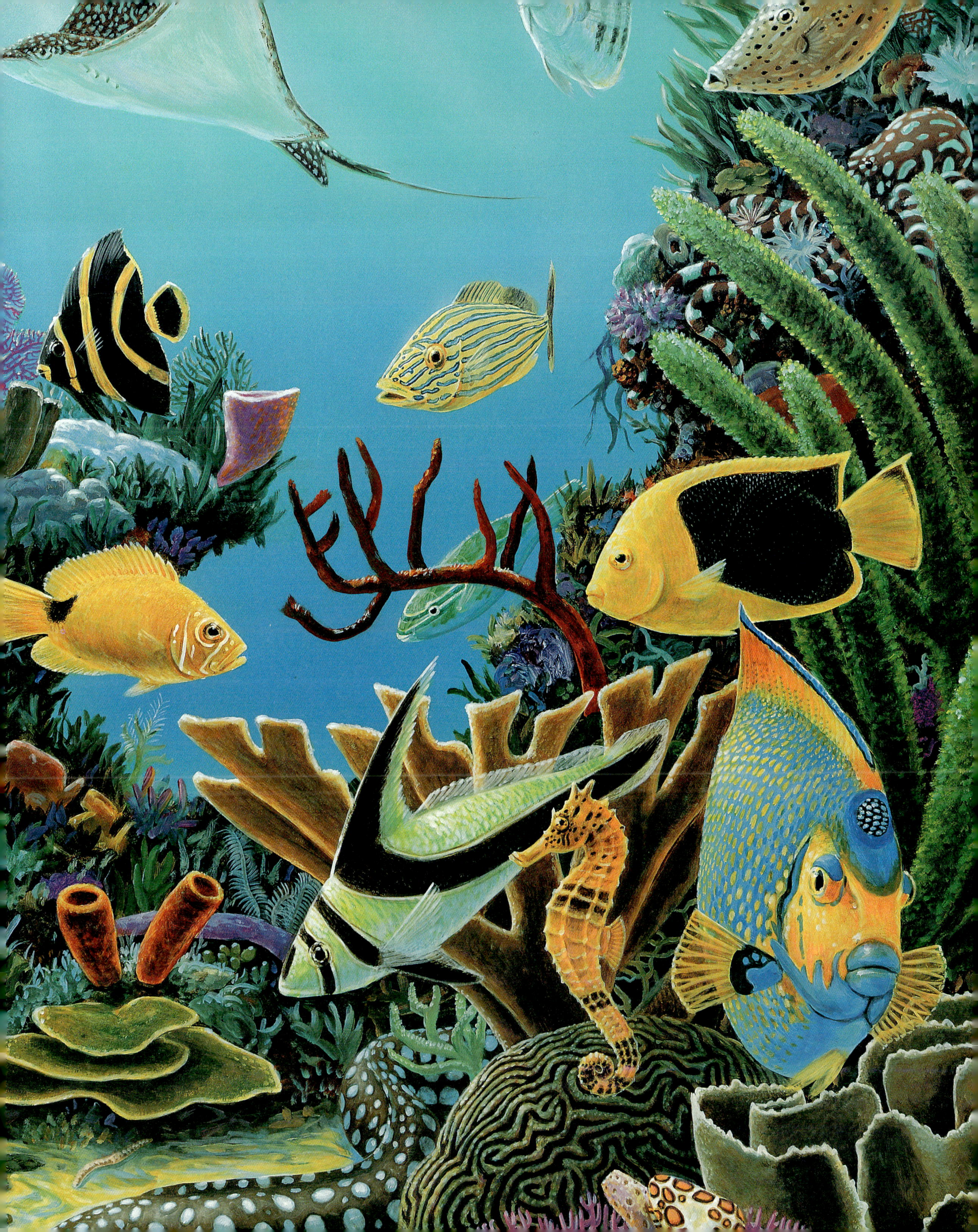

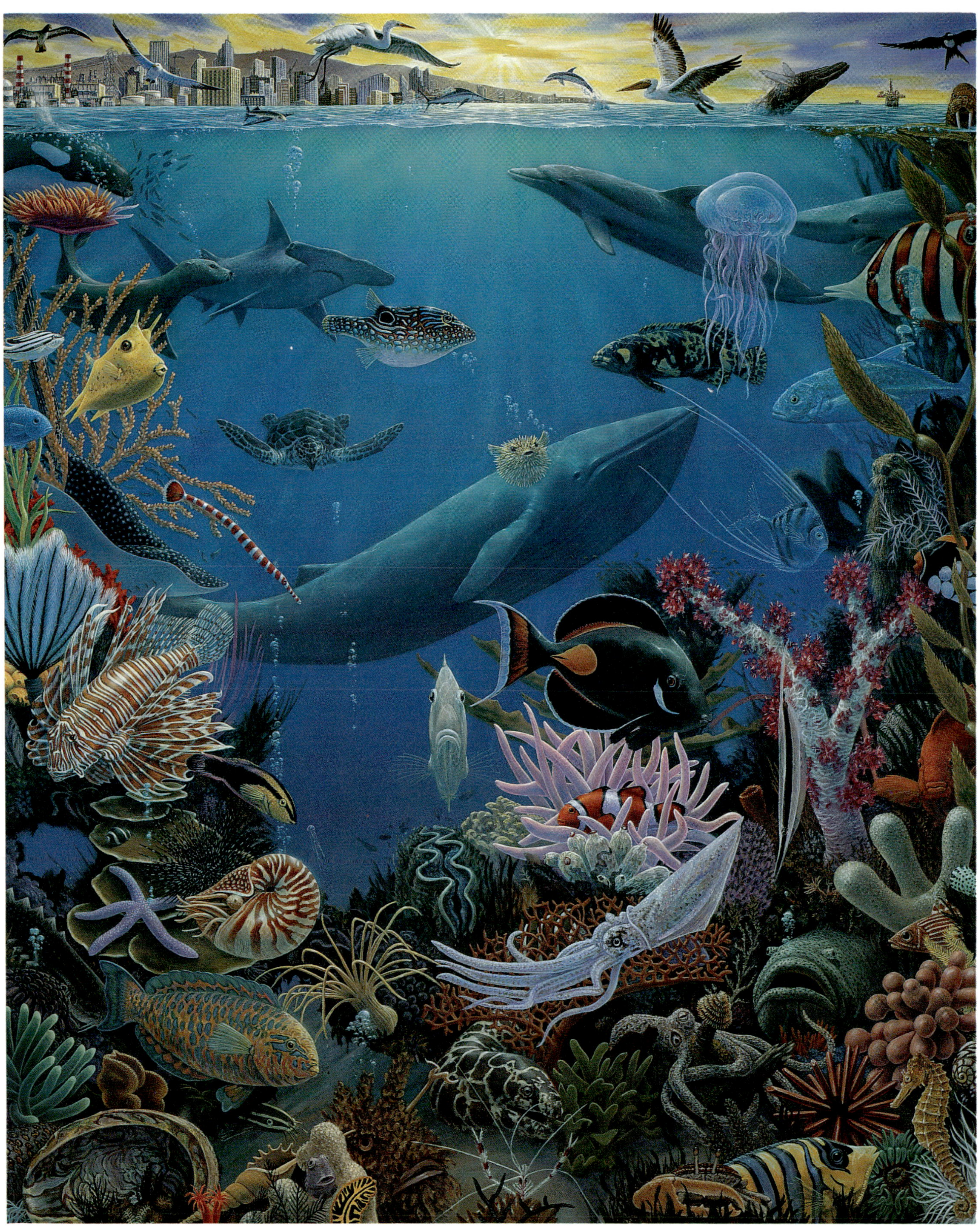

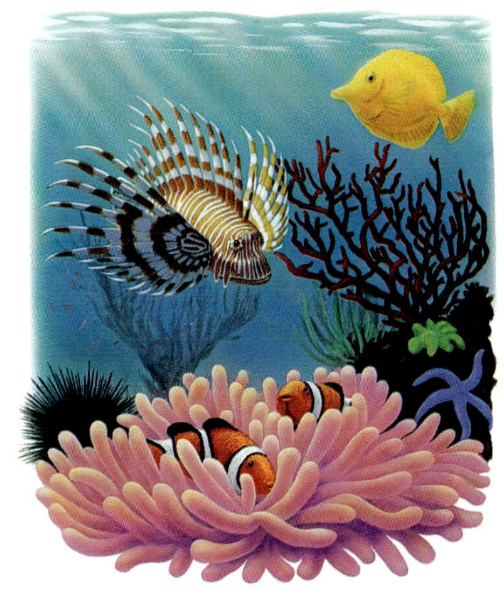

The Lion and the Clowns

1990, acrylic on canvas, 20 x 16 in.

Rescue the Reefs

1992, acrylic on canvas, 20 x 24 in.

(Previous spread)

This painting was commissioned jointly by The Nature Company and The Nature Conservancy as part of a campaign to raise money for the protection and restoration of reefs around the world. I designed the painting so that the left side of the image represents Indian and Pacific Ocean sea life and the right side represents the Atlantic and the Caribbean. The image was reproduced on posters, limited editions, jigsaw puzzles, T-shirts, greeting cards, coffee mugs, tote bags, jewelry, and note pads, and sold through The Nature Company's retail outlets and their catalogs. The sale of these products was very successful in generating money for reef restorations.

Waters' Edge

1988, acrylic on canvas, 48 x 40 in.

(Opposite)

The theme has already been done, but if I get interesting character into the creatures I'm painting, then it comes alive and fresh for me. At first, starting another one of my environmental landscapes just seems to me like a project. Go load those boxes into the truck. But then I start to see the life in the animals. Sometimes the result surprises even me.

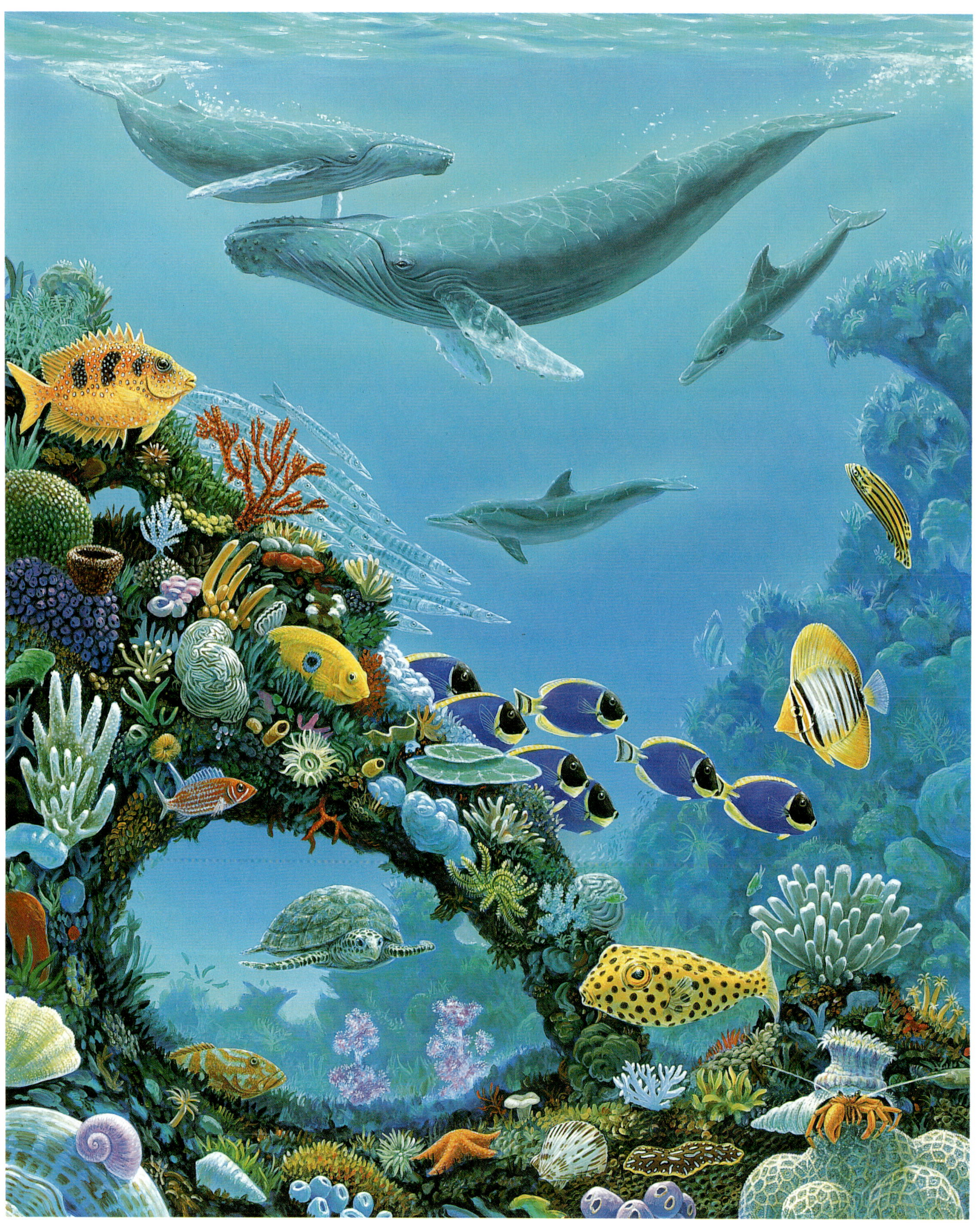

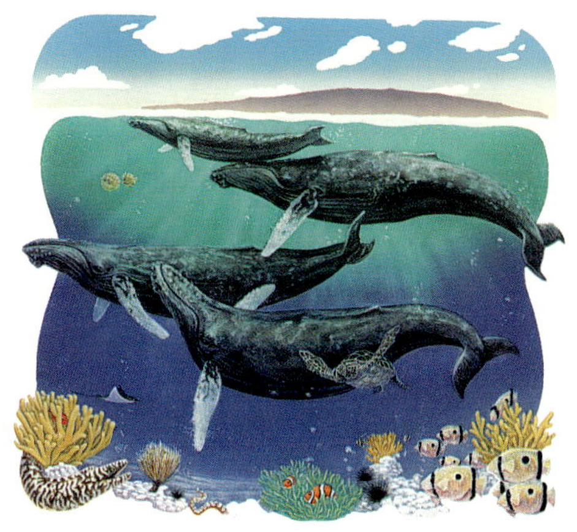

Whale's Song

1984, hand-colored etching, 30 x 24 in.

Beauty and the Reef

1993, acrylic on canvas, 20 x 16 in.

Tropical Pacific waters. Hump-back whales and bottle-nose dolphins. All kinds of reef fish—and a little turtle down below, getting "tubed," as he surf swims his way through the underwater cave.

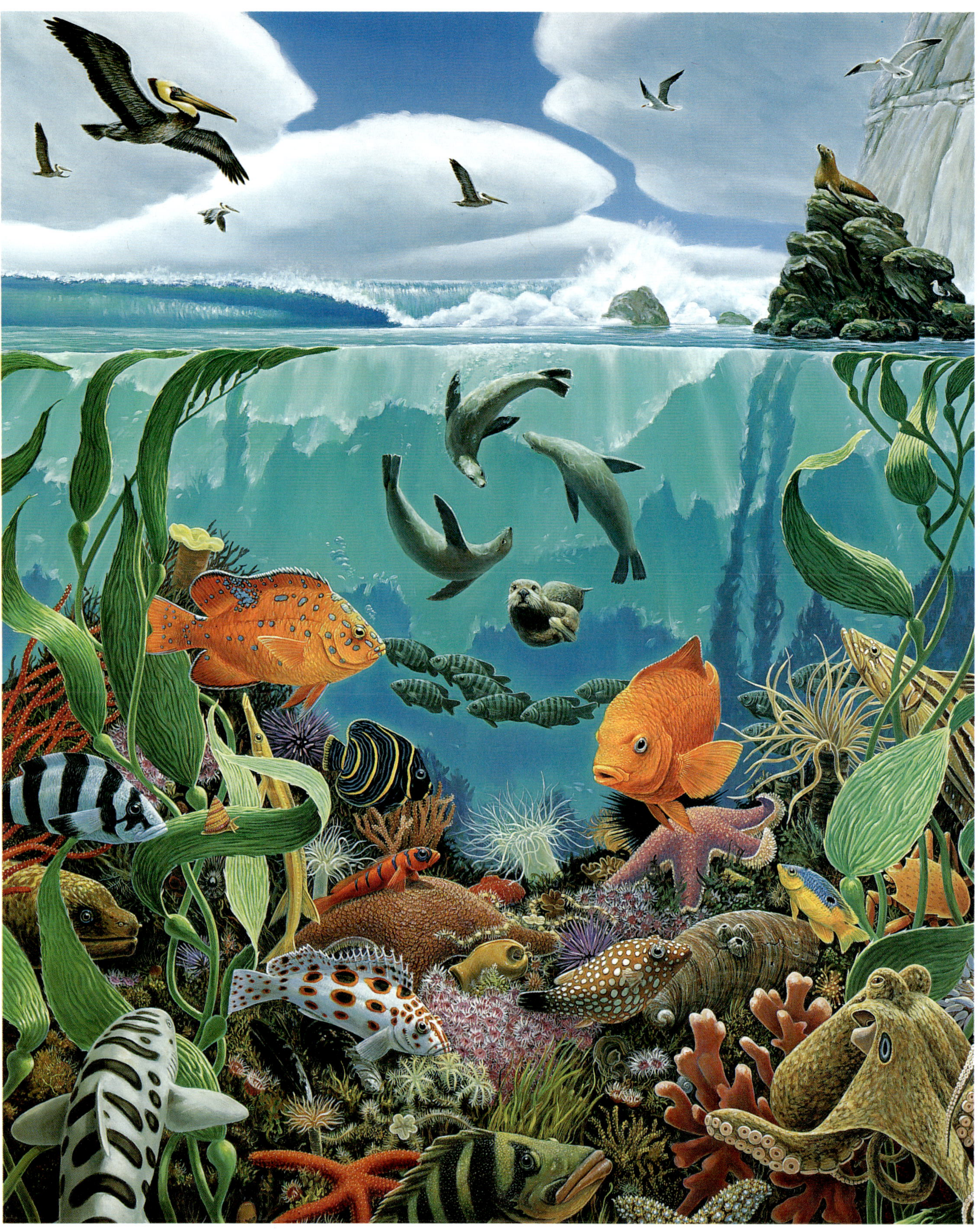

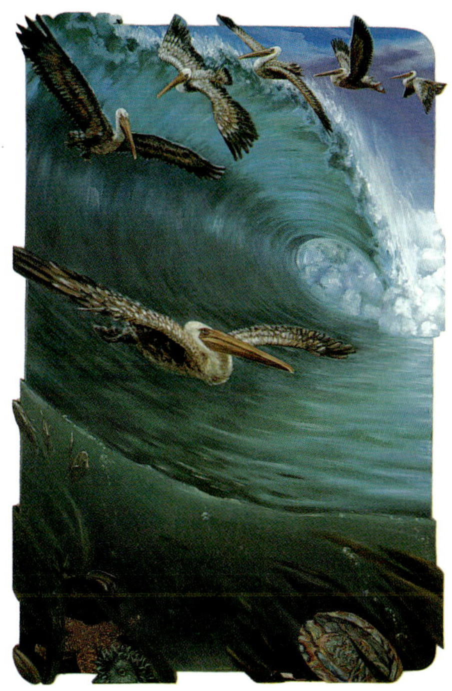

Wave

1988, oil on panel, 50 x 34 in.

California Roll

1993, acrylic and oil on canvas, 36 x 30 in.

In this painting I tried to communicate some of the many feelings I have about the ocean and the sea life off the California coast. I have spent hundreds, if not thousands, of hours in the waters of California from north of San Francisco to Magdalena Bay in Baja California, Mexico. I love surfing the waves and watching squadrons of pelicans swoop by and pods of dolphins cruise the surf zone. Many times I have seen the bright orange colors of the Garibaldi fish flashing by under my surfboard. I have been stung by jellyfish and once had a purple octopus attach itself to my arm as I was paddling out to the surf. I have seen seals basking on the beach and chasing each other in the water, and sea otters diving for their dinner. I have been entangled in the kelp and jabbed by sea urchins, picked shells on the beach, and explored the tidal pools.

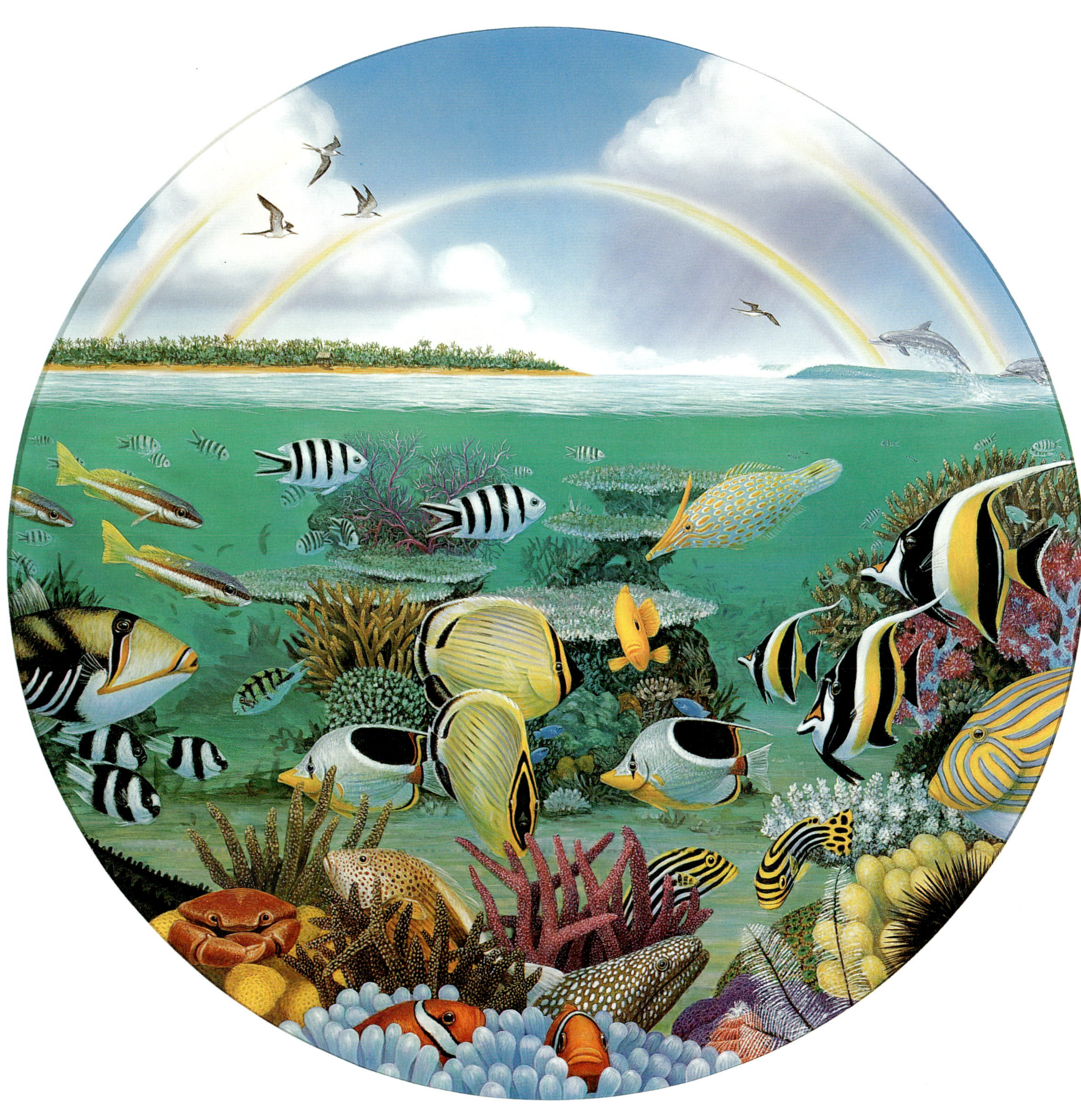

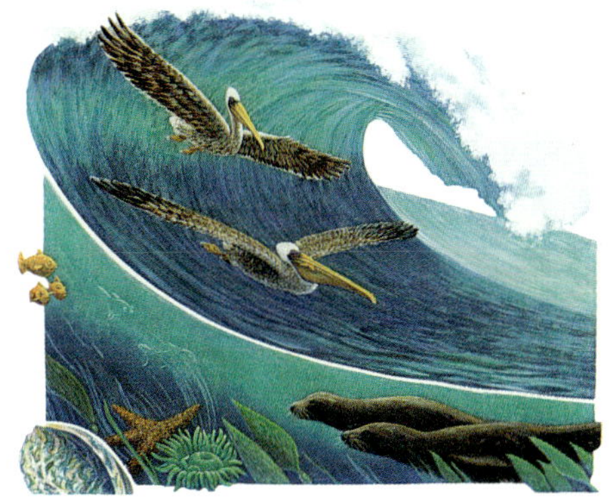

Wave

1986, hand-colored etching, 26 x 24 in.

Rainbow Reef

1991, acrylic on canvas, D: 21 in.

I have visited the island of Tavarua, Fiji, many times to surf the great waves there, dive the beautiful reefs, and get away from the hyper pace of life in Los Angeles. One afternoon, after surfing an outer reef known as Cloud Break, I was heading for safe anchorage and saw a double rainbow embracing the island. One end of the rainbow was right over perfect waves peeling across the reef, and the other end was right over the center of the island where Ratu Kini Jioji Vosa Ilagi, a once powerful chieftain of Fiji, is buried. It was spectacular and poetic. I told Scott Funk, my friend and boat driver, that someday I was going to paint that scene. And so I did.

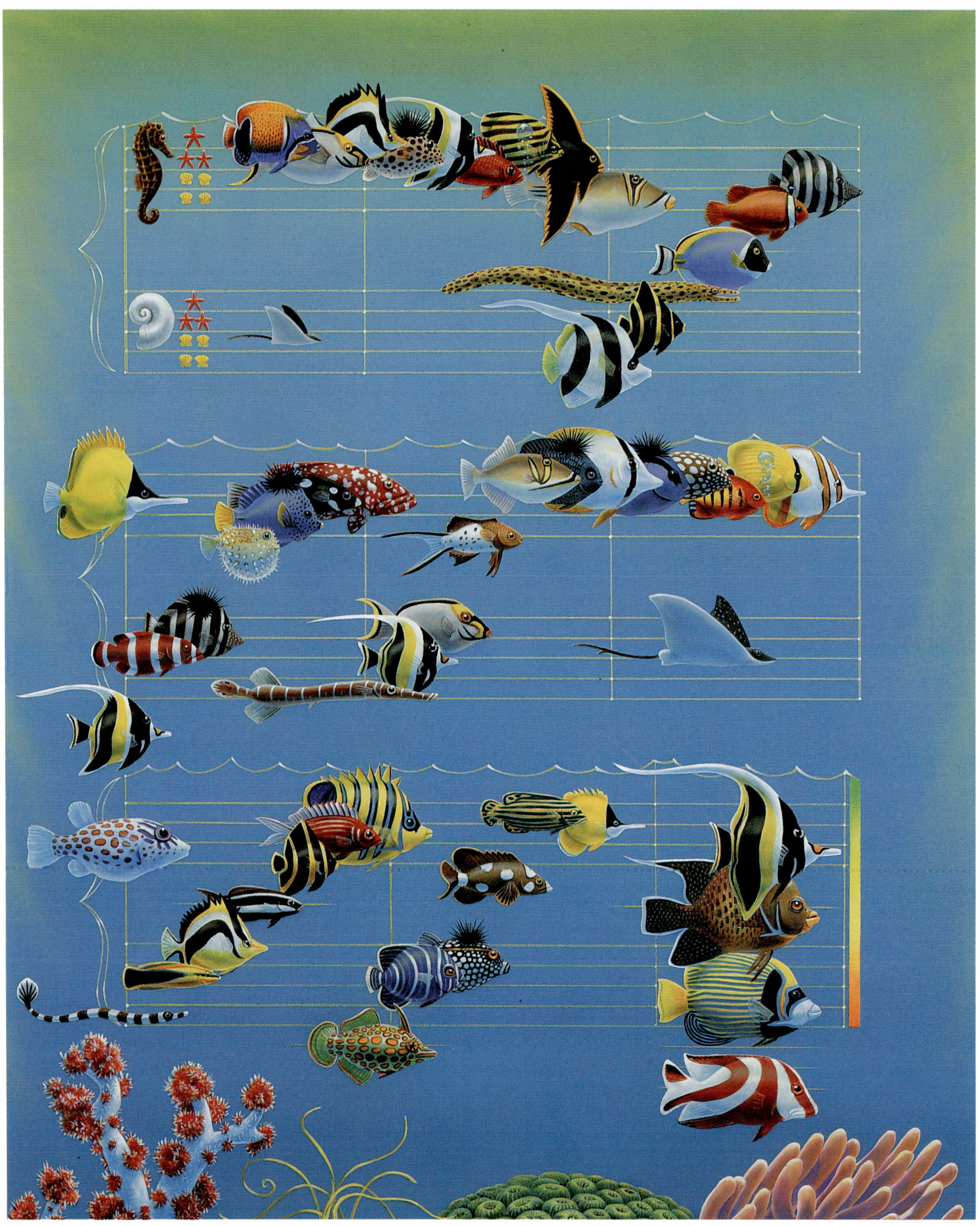

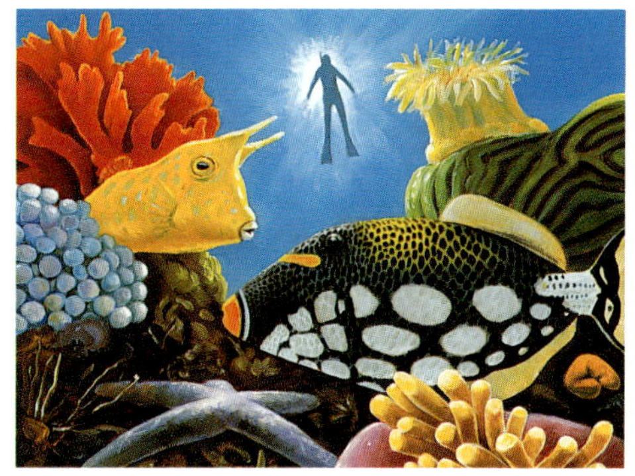

Water Space

1993, acrylic and oil on canvas, 8 x 10 in.

Musical Fish

1994, acrylic on board, 30 x 24 in.

In the spring of 1994 I was scuba diving off the coast of Bali, Indonesia, and as I watched the incredible array of colored fish floating in front of me, they seemed to be choreographed and balanced in perfect harmony. It was dazzling and inspiring. Later that afternoon, with that vision still in my mind, I thought about setting the colorful fish parade to music. I made a few sketches and came upon the idea of using fish icons to represent the notes in a musical score. Back home in my studio I made a few more sketches, including some computer-graphic versions, before I began the painting. I also chose a popular melody, which most beginning piano students will easily recognize: *Für Elise* by Ludwig van Beethoven. This is an idea I want to develop further to include animals, flowers, stars, galaxies, and so on—using them to replace the standard musical notation we're all familiar with.

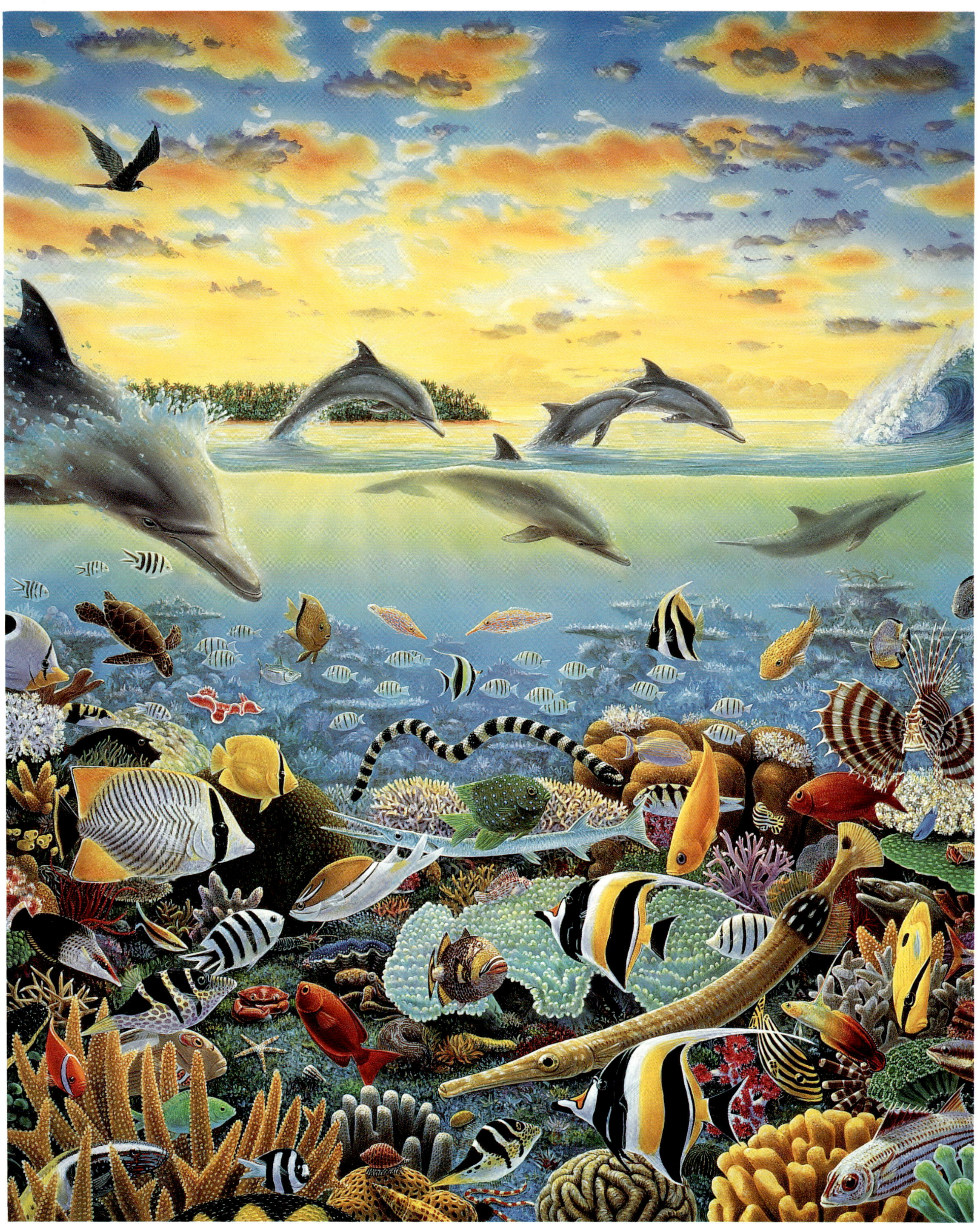

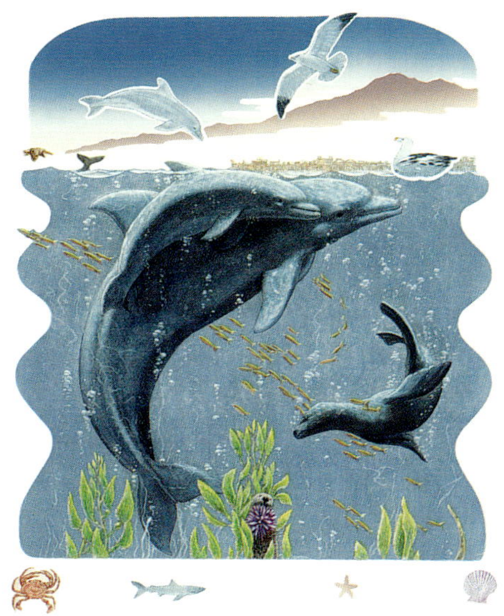

Dolphins and Friends

1983, hand-colored etching, 32 x 24 in.

Tales of Tavarua

1991, acrylic on canvas, 48 x 40 in.

Tavarua is a very small outer island of Fiji, which I have visited five times. I go there to surf the great waves, dive in the warm clear water, and reacquaint myself with the wonderful friends I have made there. The painting does not exaggerate the diversity or density of animal and plant life. Just a few short yards off the beach, you find the spectacular array of fish, coral, and other sea life I have depicted in my painting.

Druku is the current chief of the local community. His great-grandfather was a great chief of many island communities and is buried at the very center of Tavarua. To honor both Druku and his great-grandfather, I painted their faces in the clouds, and the great-grandfather's face is also the basis for the positioning of many of the fish. For example, the jumping dolphins are his eyelids, the two blue-spotted filefish are his nostrils, the sea snake is the upper line of his lips. Can you find the rest of him?

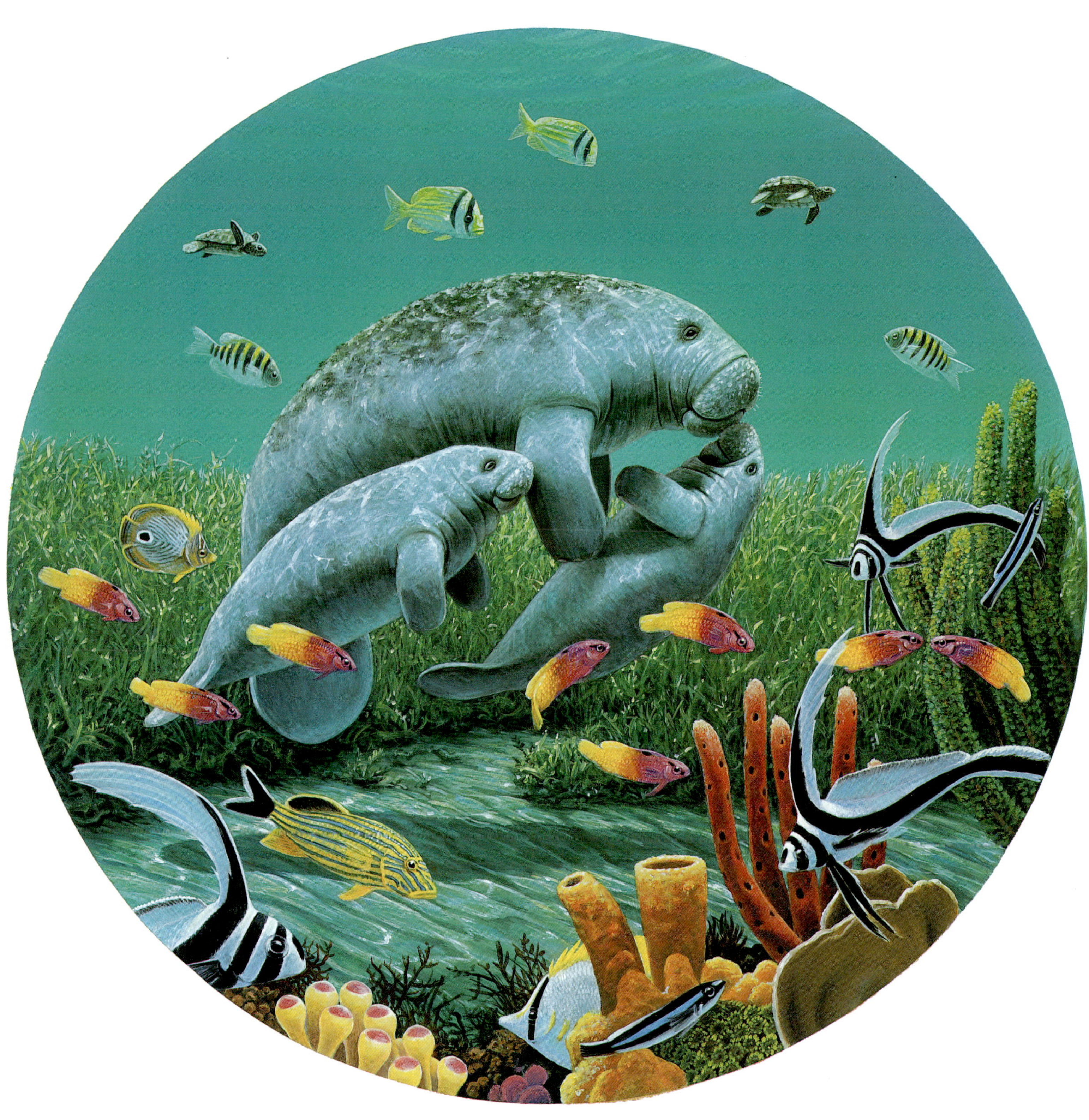

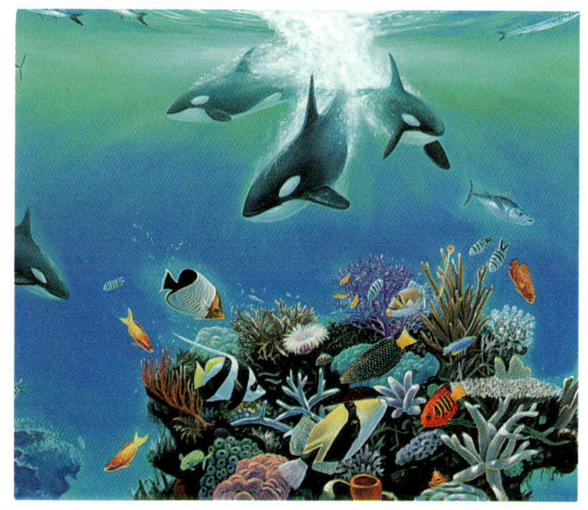

Orca Blues

1993, acrylic and oil on canvas, 18 x 24 in.

Manatee Moments

1993, acrylic and oil on board, D: 16 in.

I have never seen a manatee in person. I have studied many photographs and video documentaries of them, and I find them endearing. They are docile, friendly vegetarians. Even though they are quite large—after all, they are also called "sea cows"—they are very gentle and caring with each other. The greatest dangers they face are encounters with human beings. Pollution, loss of habitat, and getting gashed by boat propellers are the main and relentless causes of their doom. Efforts to protect them have so far met with only marginal success.

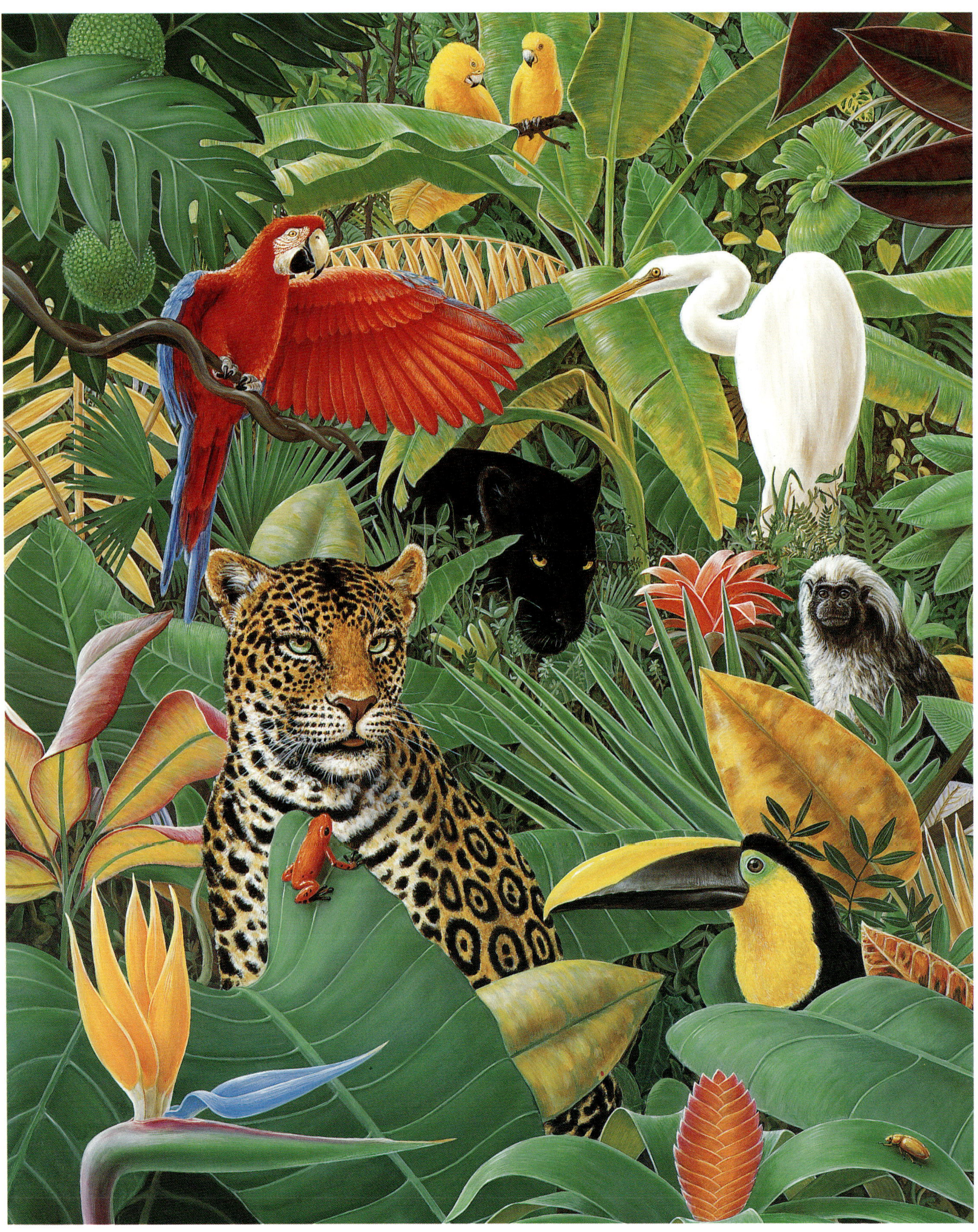

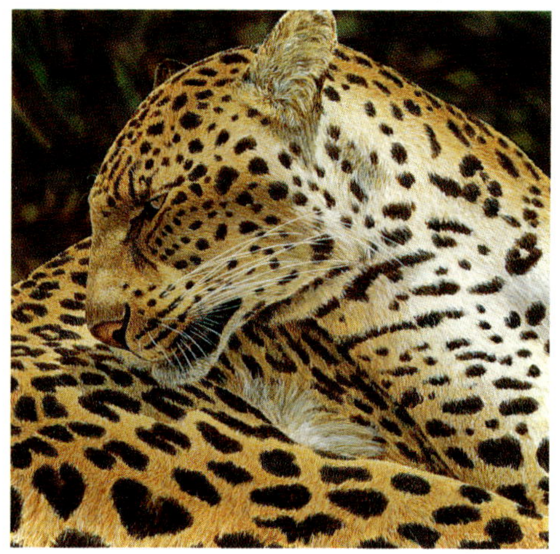

Leopard

1990, acrylic on canvas, 16 x 18 in.

Jungle Story

1992, acrylic on canvas, 30 x 24 in.

This was going to be on the cover of a college biology/ecology textbook. I didn't feel attached to the painting at first. I felt like I wasn't being artistic. I was just doing a job because it was a commission. But then, after a while, it took on a life and energy that made me really like it. The animals developed character and started coming to life. It's just paint. But sometimes things seem to come to life, and I'm really glad I painted them.

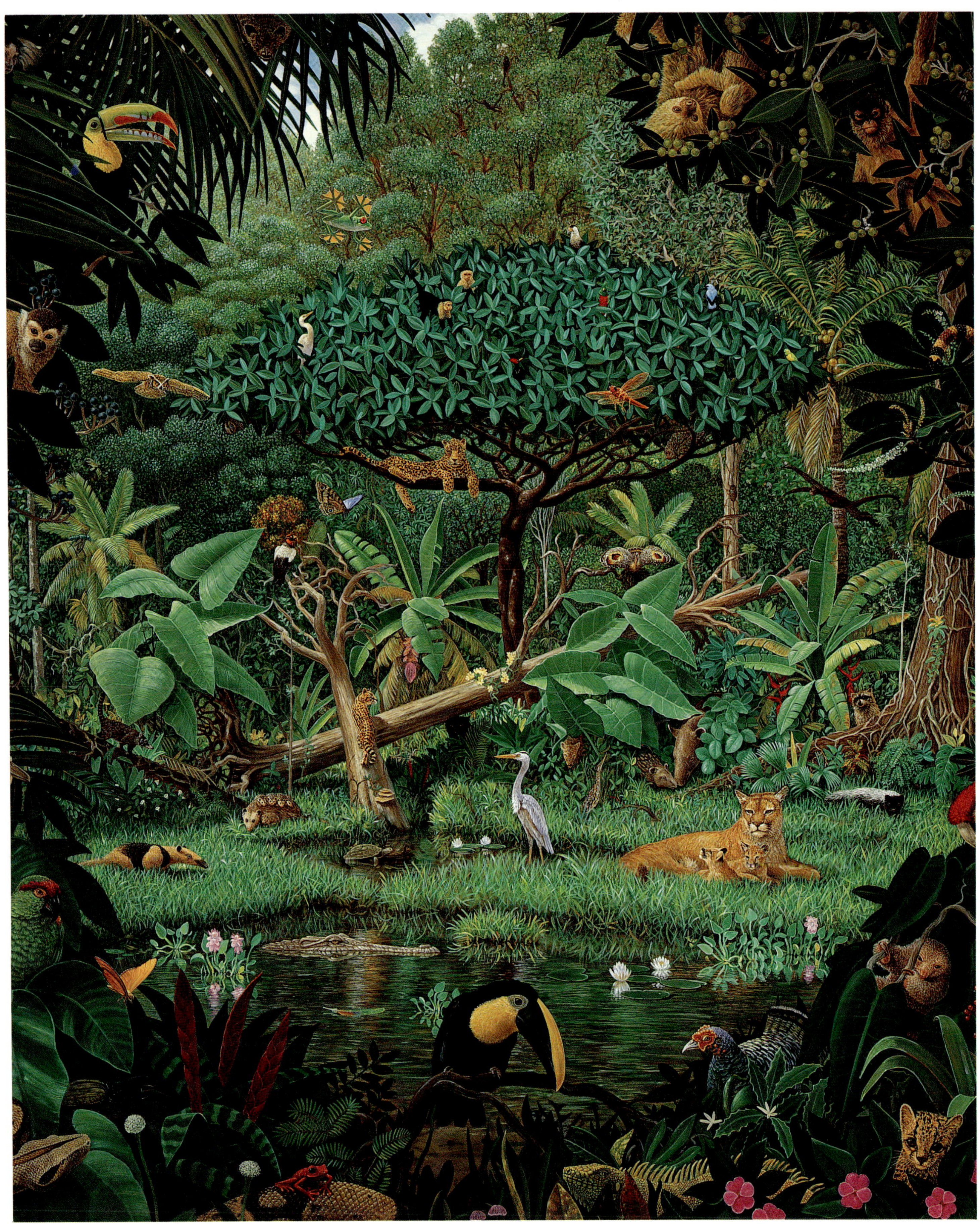

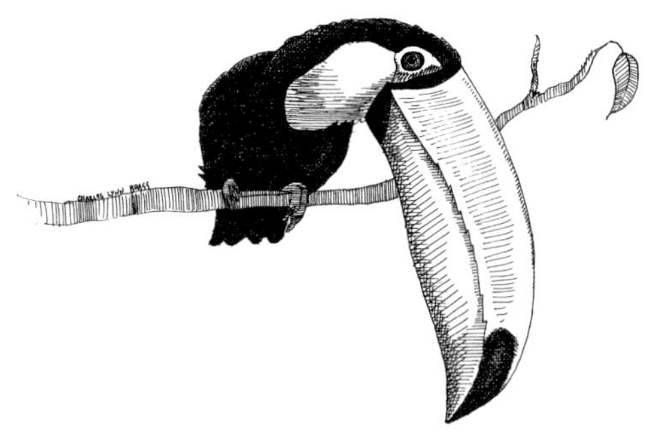

Beak Too Big Toucan

1994, ink on paper, 5 x 8 in.

Secrets of the Rainforest

1991, acrylic on canvas, 60 x 52 in.

This is a Costa Rican jungle. I went to Costa Rica in 1990 to camp and surf. I saw the toucans, the sloths, and the monkeys. The little baby ocelot in the bottom right corner was someone's pet in the lobby of the hotel. While I was working on the painting, a puzzle company saw a photograph of it and wanted an exclusive on the painting for a children's puzzle. I sent them photographs of the work in progress. I sent transparencies.

"We love it," they said.

In the midst of manufacturing the puzzle, they discovered the middle tree trunk has a female form in it. And they went crazy.

"You can't put a naked lady in a children's puzzle!"

They wanted me to paint her out, but I didn't own the painting anymore. It was long gone. So they used a computer to smoosh out the more prominent features of her anatomy. Maybe my original veers toward an R rating, but the children's puzzle version is definitely PG-13.

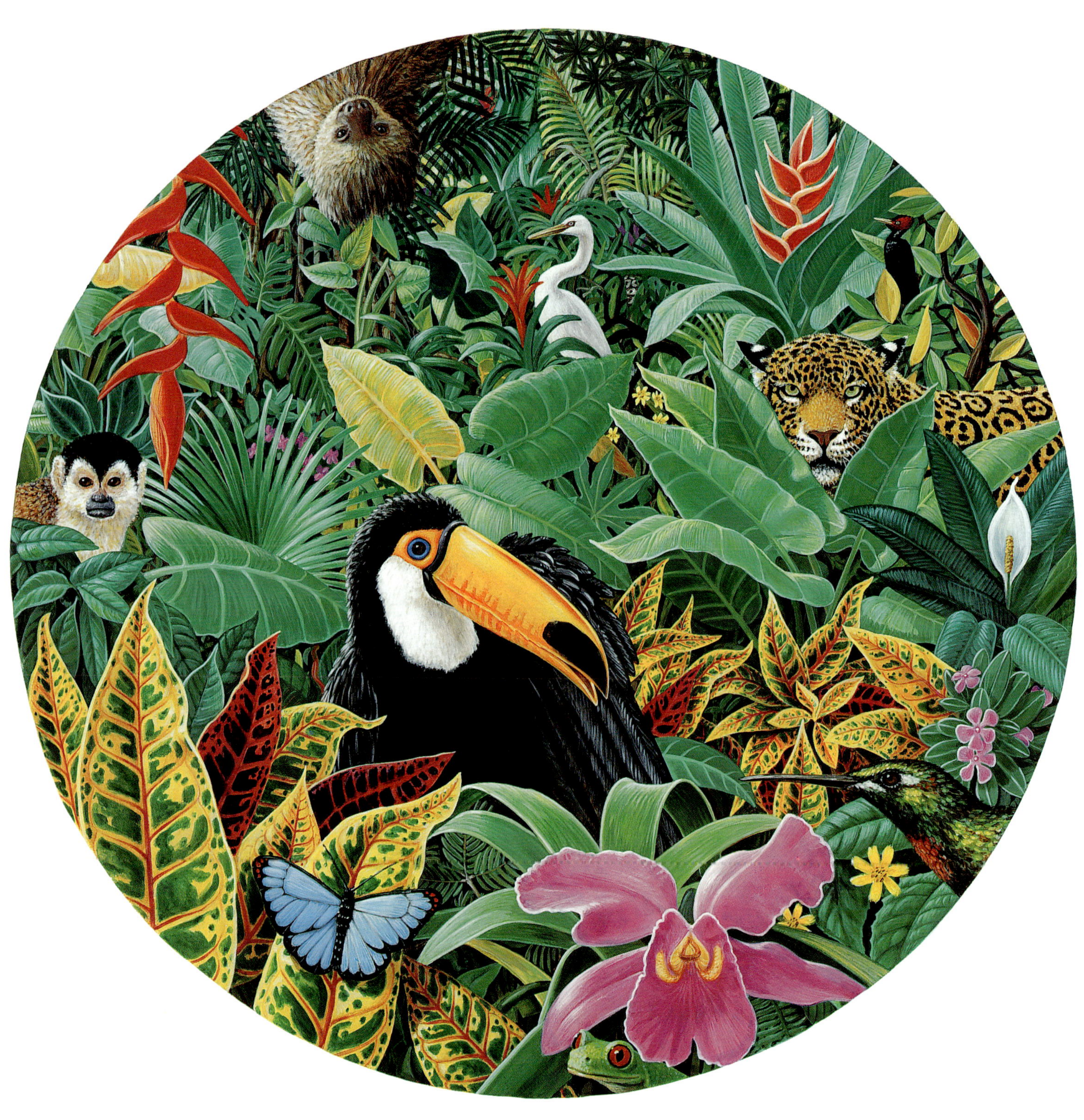

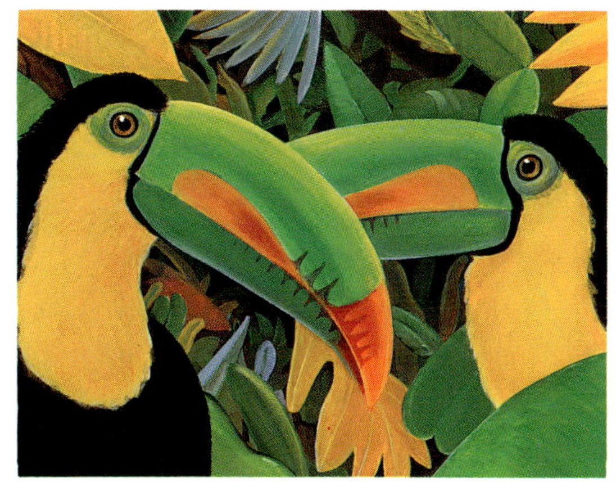

Toucan Twins

1992, acrylic on canvas, 8 x 10 in.

Rainforest Magic

1990, acrylic on canvas, D: 16 in.

When I was in Costa Rica exploring, surfing, and photographing the jungles, forests, and beaches I had heard so much about, I went on a boat expedition to Tortuguero, where the coastal canals wind their way slowly through thick jungle along the Caribbean Sea. I saw many creatures, from incredible bugs, crocodiles, iguanas, frogs, and turtles, to sloths, monkeys, toucans, eagles, and ocelots. *Rainforest Magic* is one of several paintings in which I have tried to capture the dense, diverse, and colorful array of life in Costa Rica.

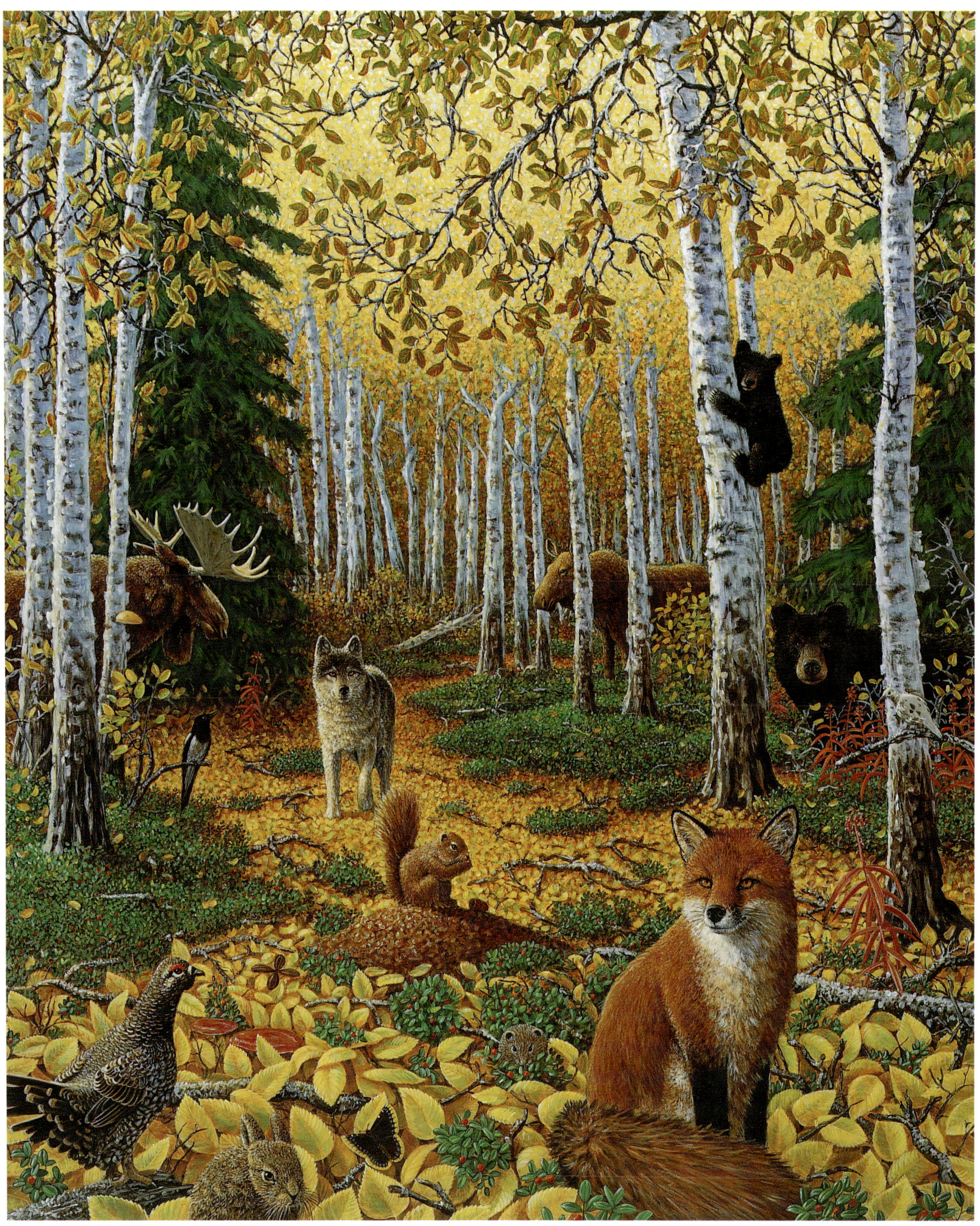

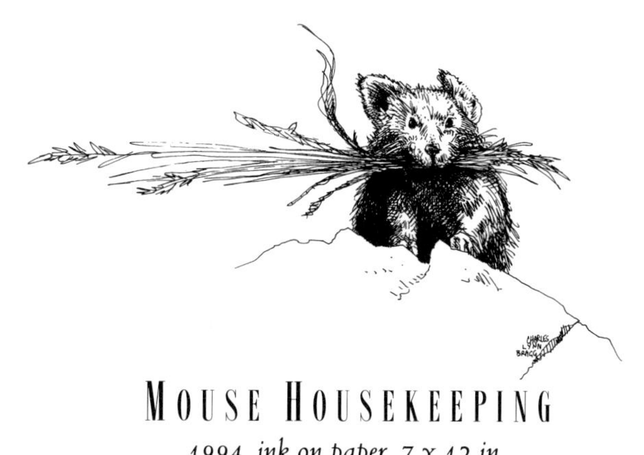

Mouse Housekeeping

1994, ink on paper, 7 x 12 in.

Alaska Autumn

1992, acrylic on paper, 30 x 24 in.

I went to Alaska and hired a guide who took me by waterplane and canoe into the wilderness. It was fall, which is a very short season that far north. The birch leaves had turned a brilliant yellow. We saw lots of caribou, moose, geese, and a black bear. It was hard to decide what I should focus on. As I painted, it changed over and over again until the painting said *This is the way it's going to be.*

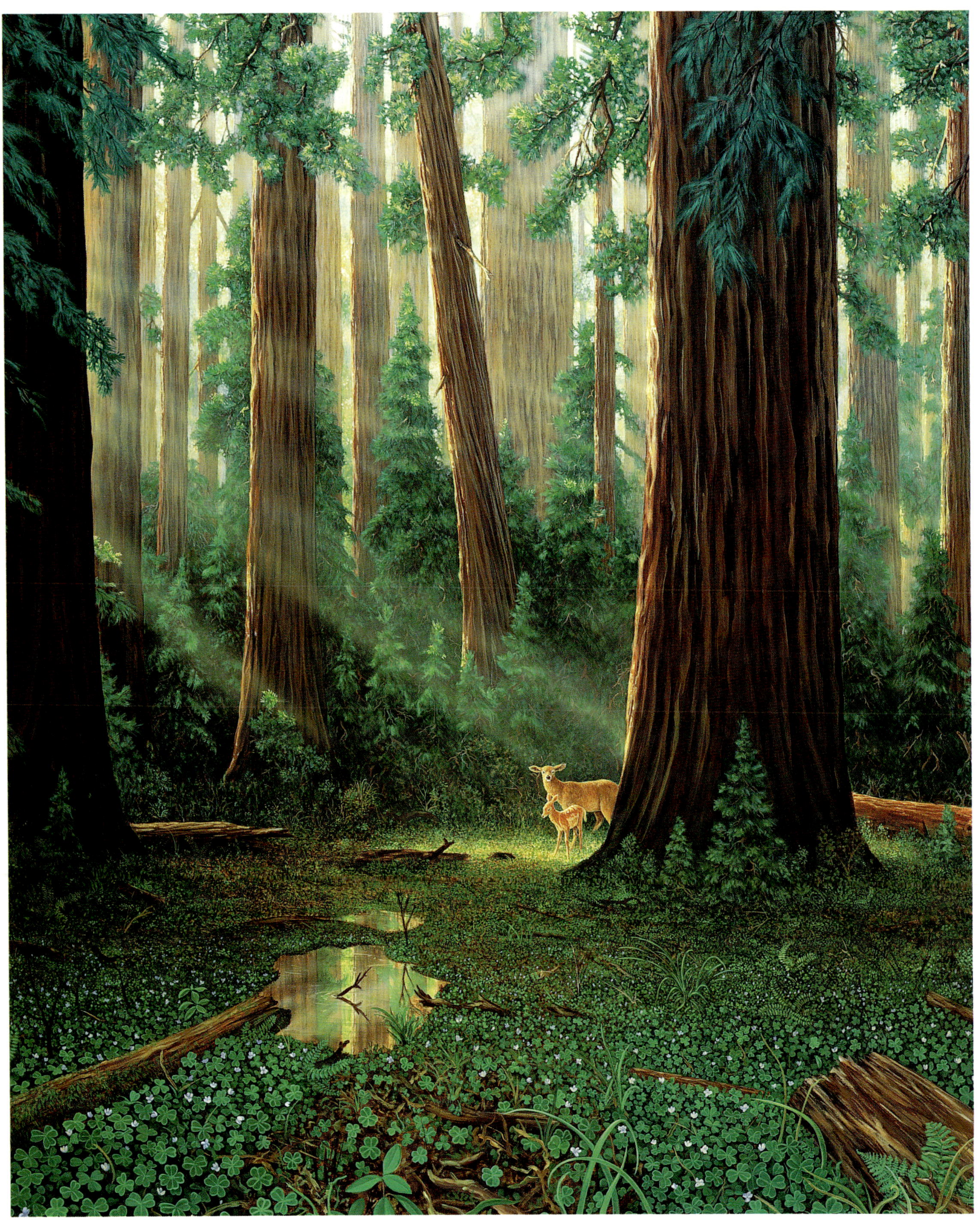

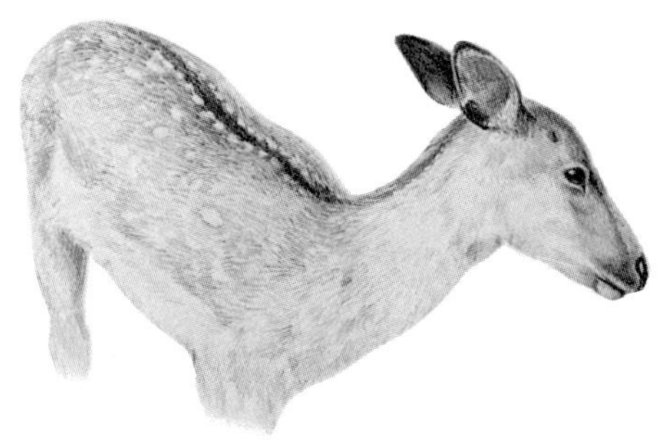

Fawn

1993, pencil on paper, 8 x 10 in.

The Last Stand

1989, acrylic on canvas, 48 x 40 in.

It was 1989. I had done *City Limits*, *Waters' Edge*, and *Last Oasis*. They were so filled with animals and they took me so long that I thought I would do a scene with just a couple of animals in it and see if that would be easier. It still took me just as long to do it.

There is one four-leaf clover, and it's up to you to find it. I'm not telling.

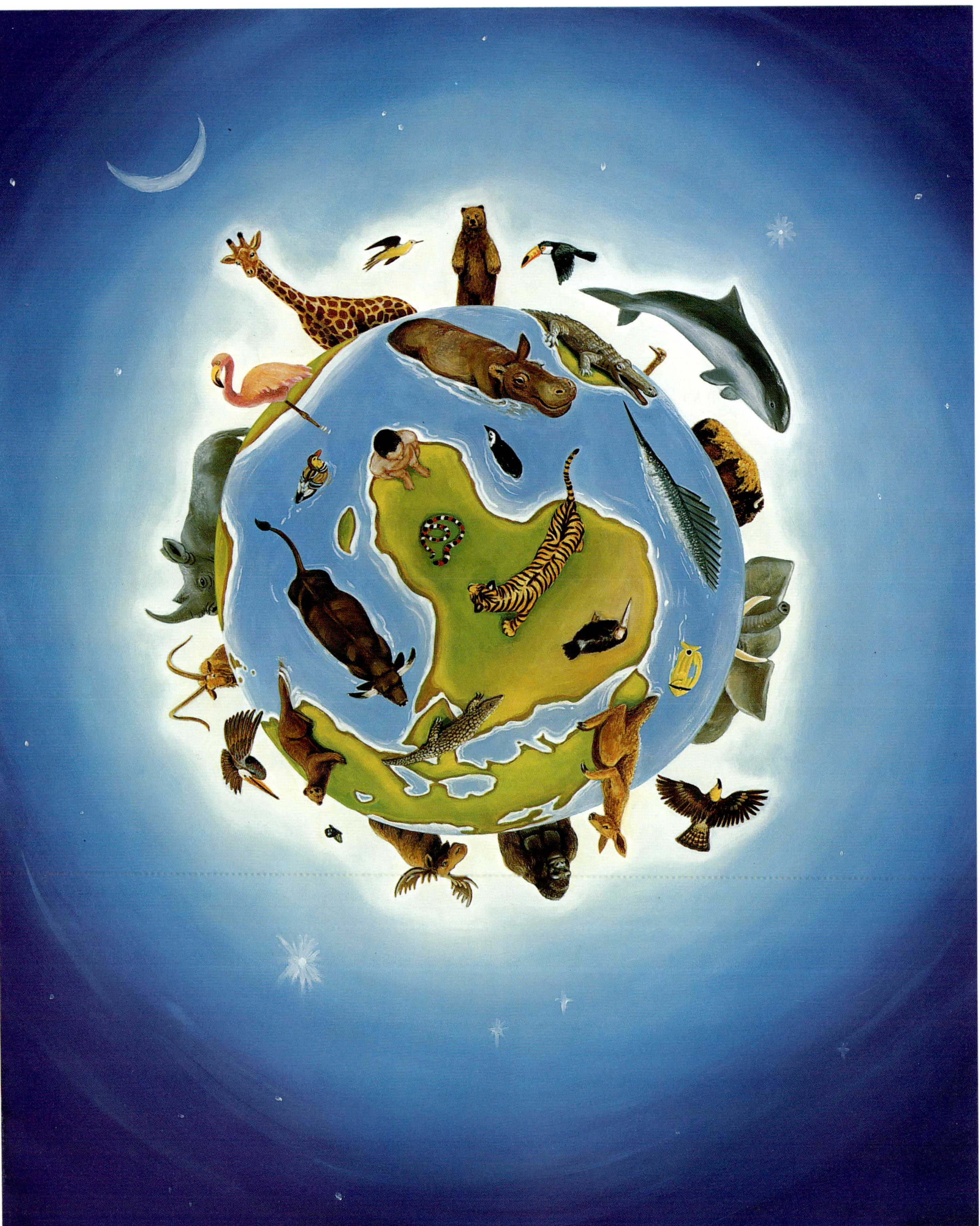

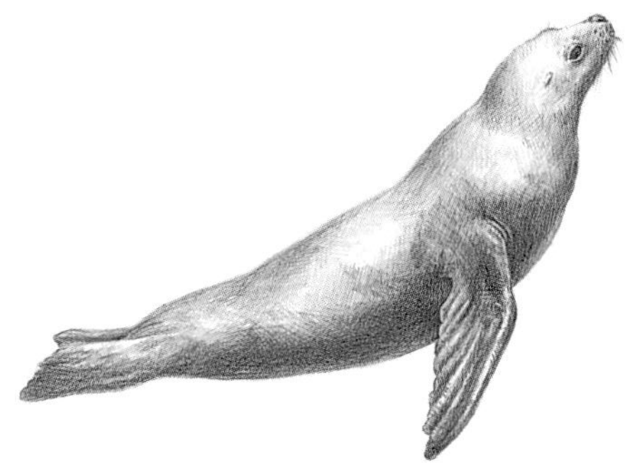

Seal

1993, pencil on paper, 8 x 10 in.

The Shrinking Planet

1993, acrylic/oil on canvas, 20 x 16 in.

A little planet with creatures on it, finding out how close they really are to each other. I kept thinking of mottoes when I did this: *Conserve and Preserve.* Or: *Protect and Respect.*

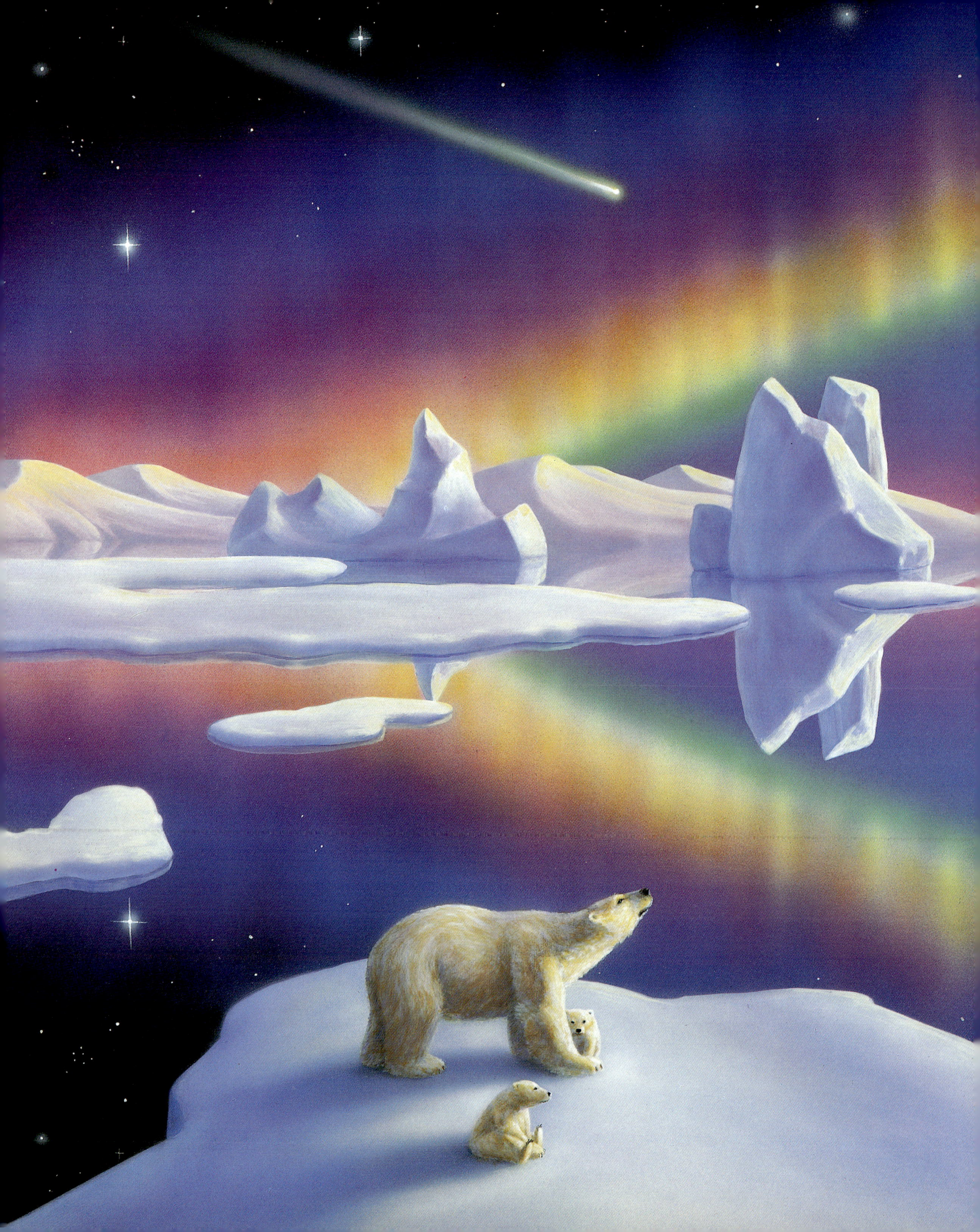

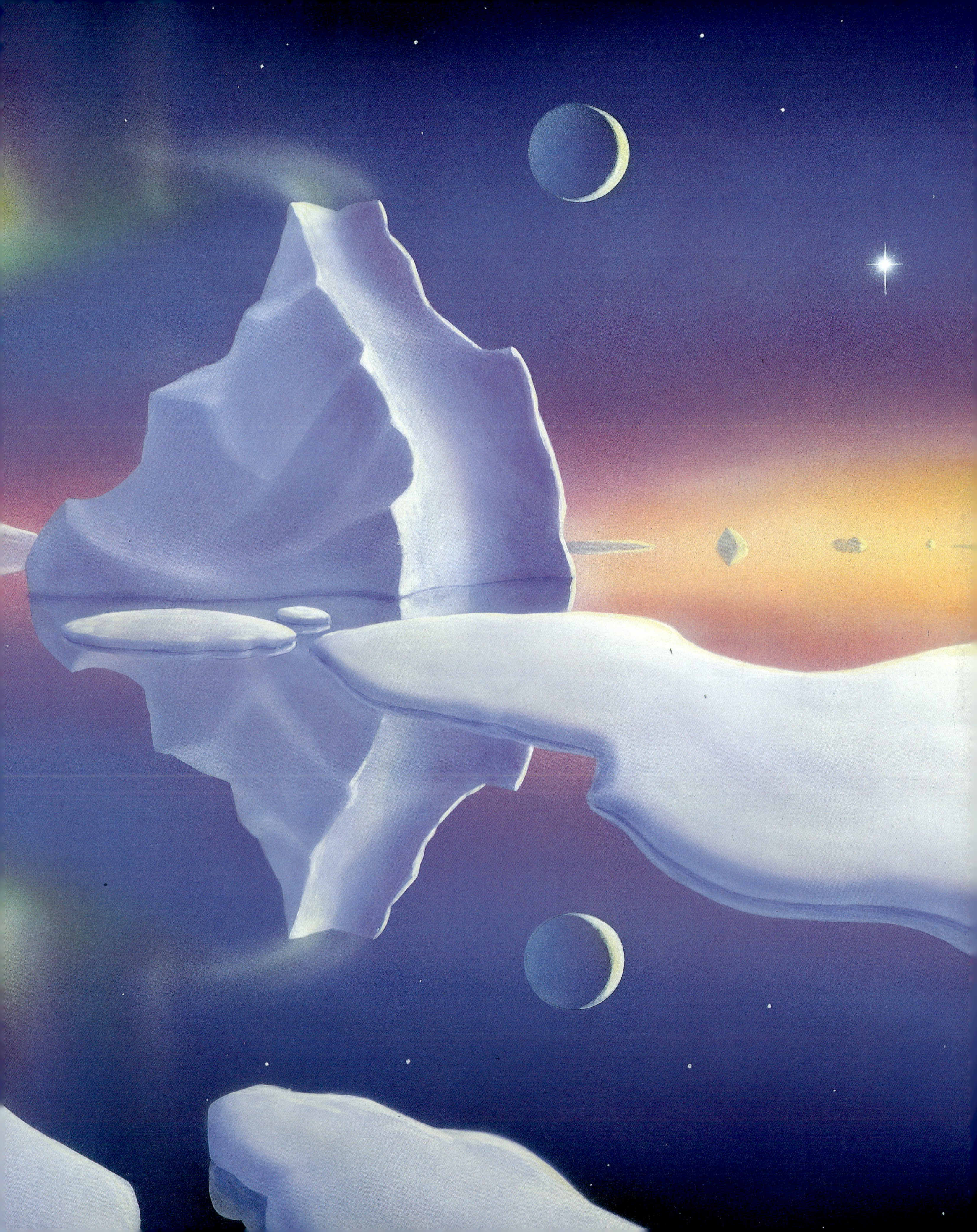

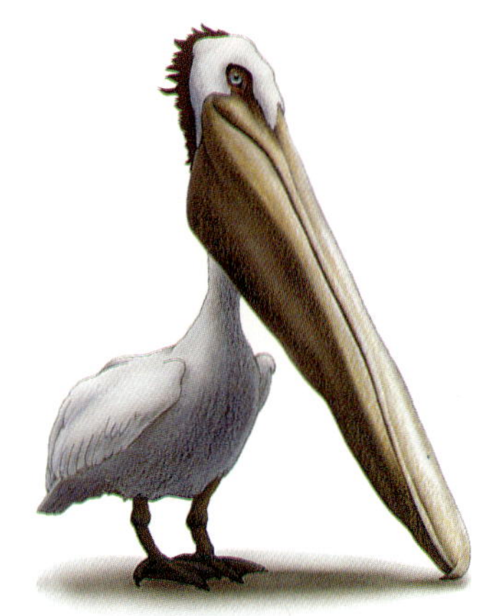

El Pico (Pelican)

1994, ink and colored pencil, 16 x 12 in.

Legend of Aurora

1994, acrylic on linen, 24 x 30 in.
(Previous spread)

This work was commissioned by the head of a Japanese firm who wanted an image of a polar bear and her cubs with an aurora borealis. I made several thumbnail sketches, which I faxed to my client. He chose the design he liked best, and I began to paint. Two weeks later, I sent him a photograph of what I had done. He wanted the aurora changed. Even though I was quite satisfied with the one I had already painted, I repainted the sky, and repainted and repainted and repainted until, finally, we were both pleased.

Museum of Natural History

1992, acrylic on canvas, 11 x 14 in.

So now we're history, and we're stuffed in the dioramas, and the animals are studying us. Each exhibit has a note describing our good points, our weaknesses, our accomplishments, and our follies.

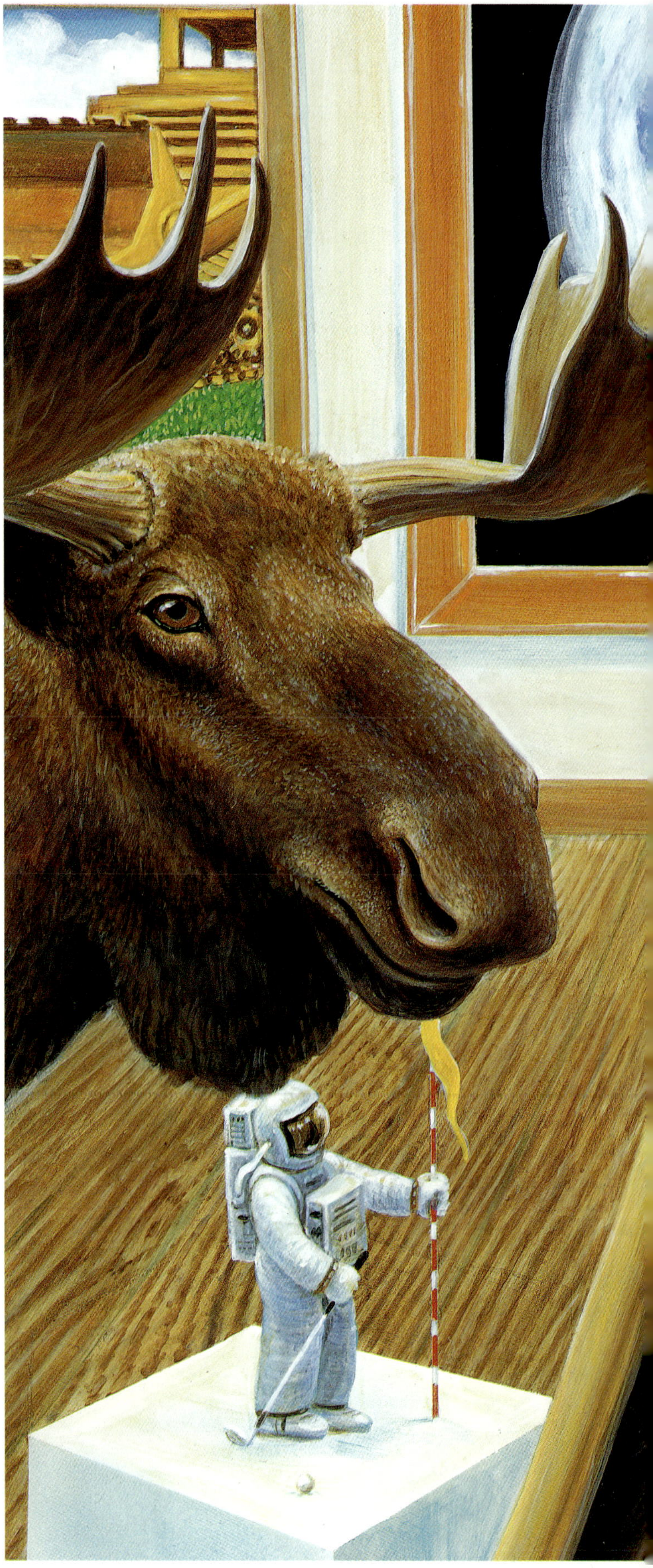

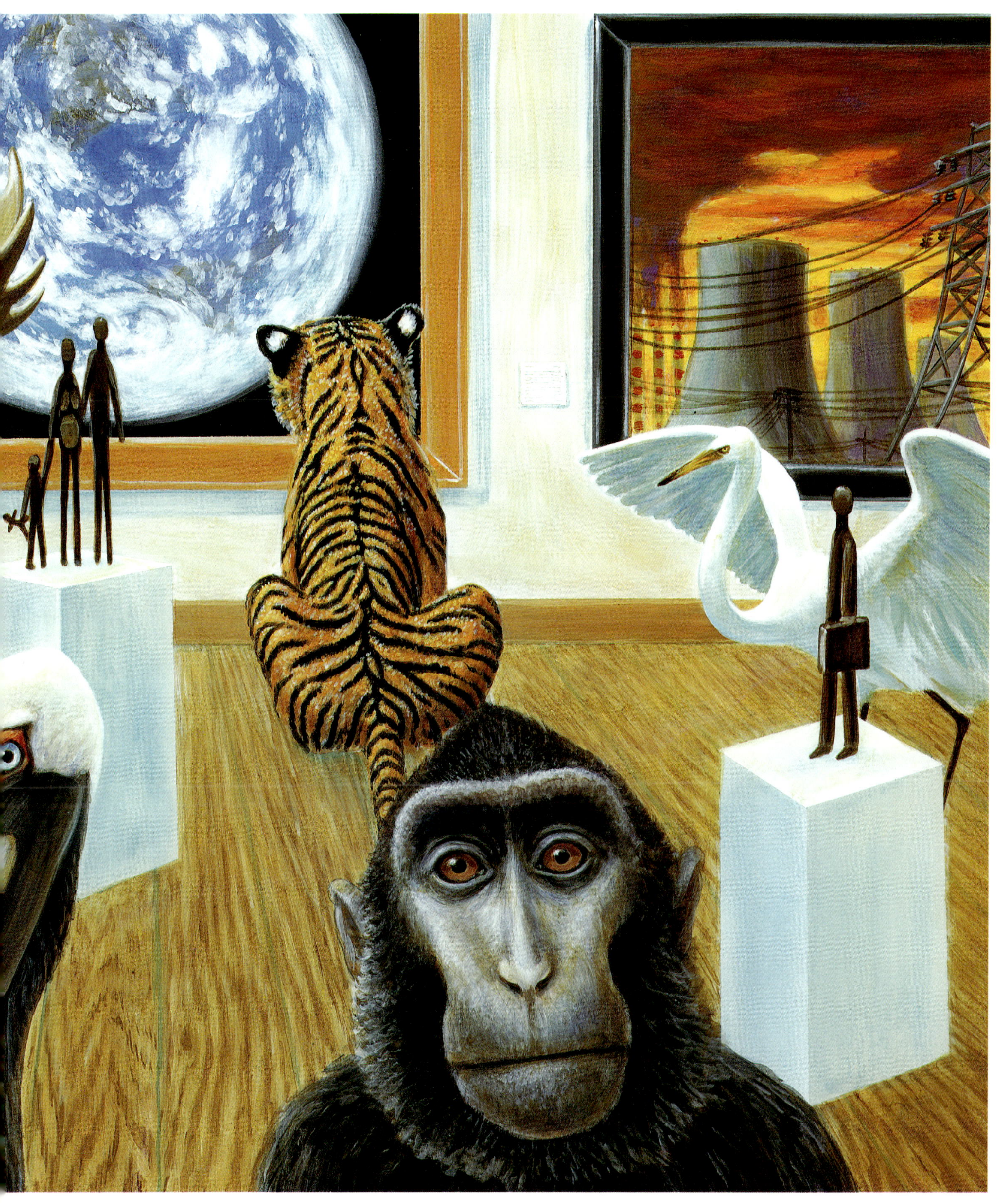

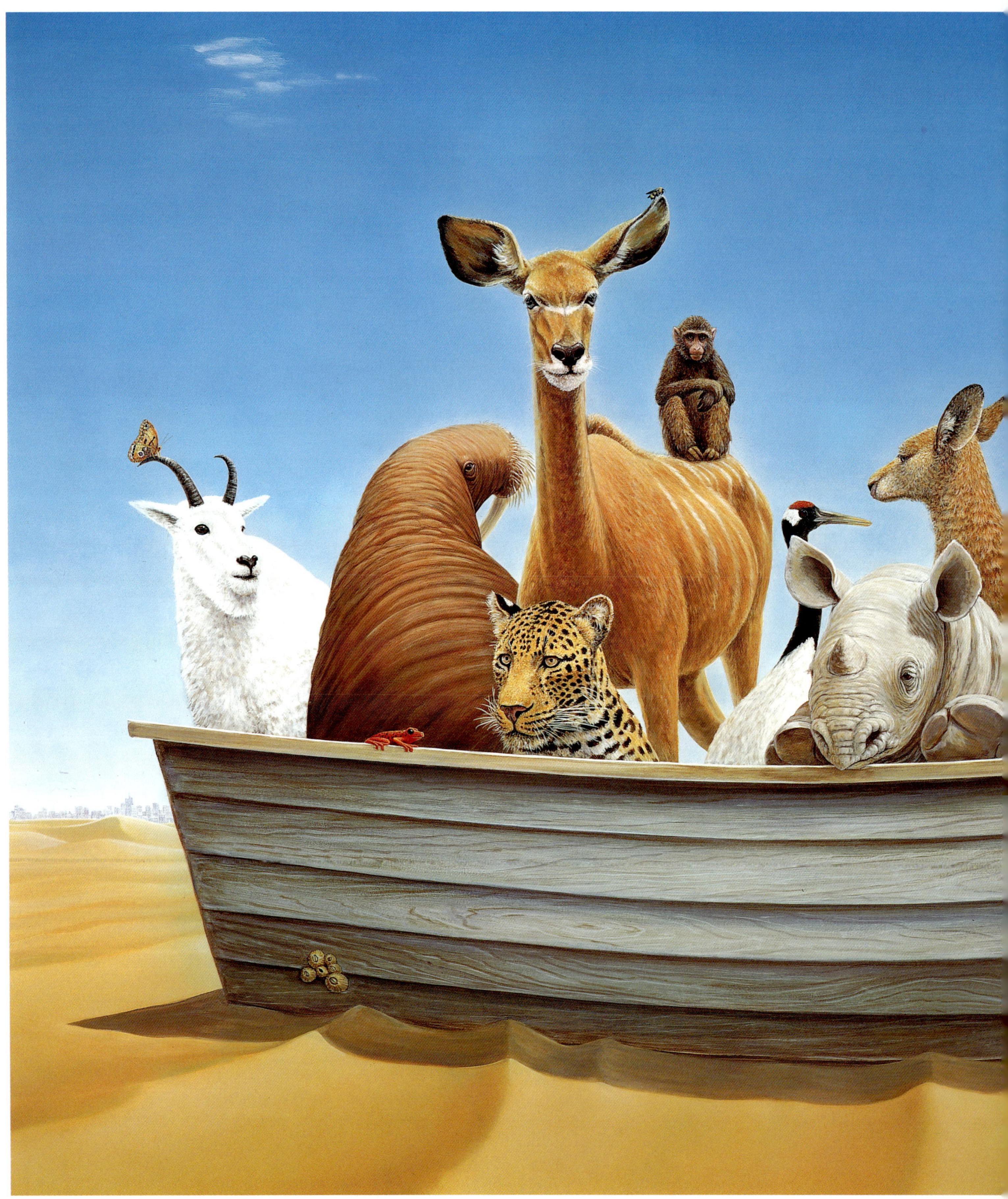

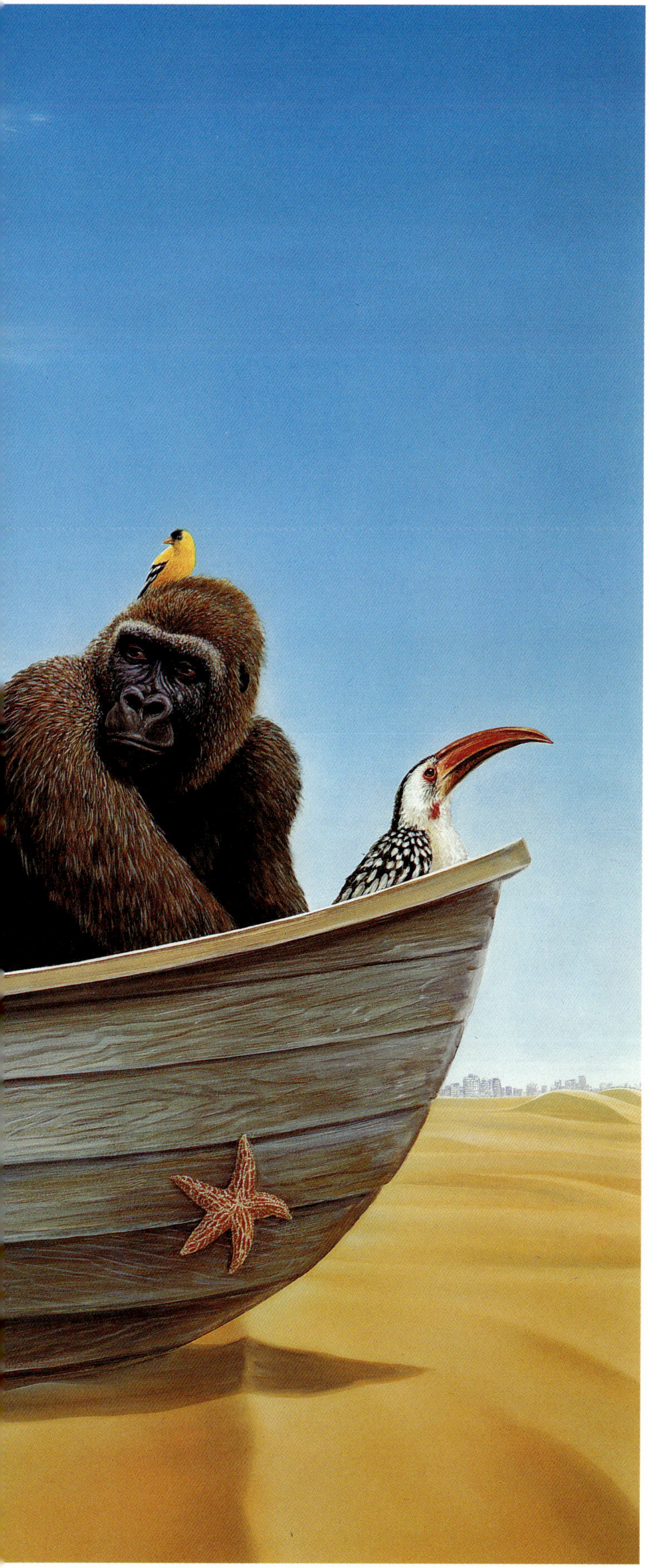

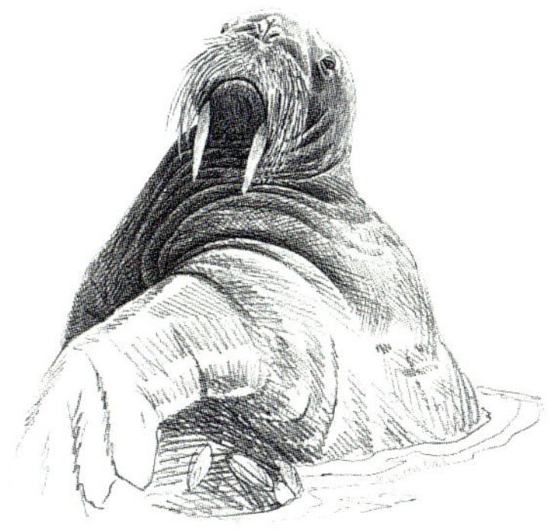

Walrus

1993, pencil, 10 x 10 in.

Bon Voyage

1991, acrylic on canvas, 48 x 72 in.

I didn't want to make it a literal Noah's Ark. I made three sketches. Two of them were this boat in the water, just water as far as you could see. No land in sight. Then I thought, "What about a boat on land?" I put the boat in the sketch, full of animals, on land: a desert.

It's a little old rickety row boat full of animals, some of which are endangered species. I'd always wanted to paint the gorilla. He was so beautiful and looked so intelligent. I just had to paint him. I was lucky enough to fit him in the boat, as if he were the key figure in there.

Cracked desert usually means the land was real wet and then dried real fast. Sand dunes have cracked and cracked and cracked, until there is just sand left. The sand looks like water because of the way the wind blows it into waves. That's how water turns into waves. Wind blows it. Sand dunes are just slow-motion waves.

The painting is 4 by 6 feet. I wanted it to have a big impact. I wanted it to be impressive. I wanted it to have a presence.

All the animals are looking in different directions. They're all in the same boat. They're all going to the same place.

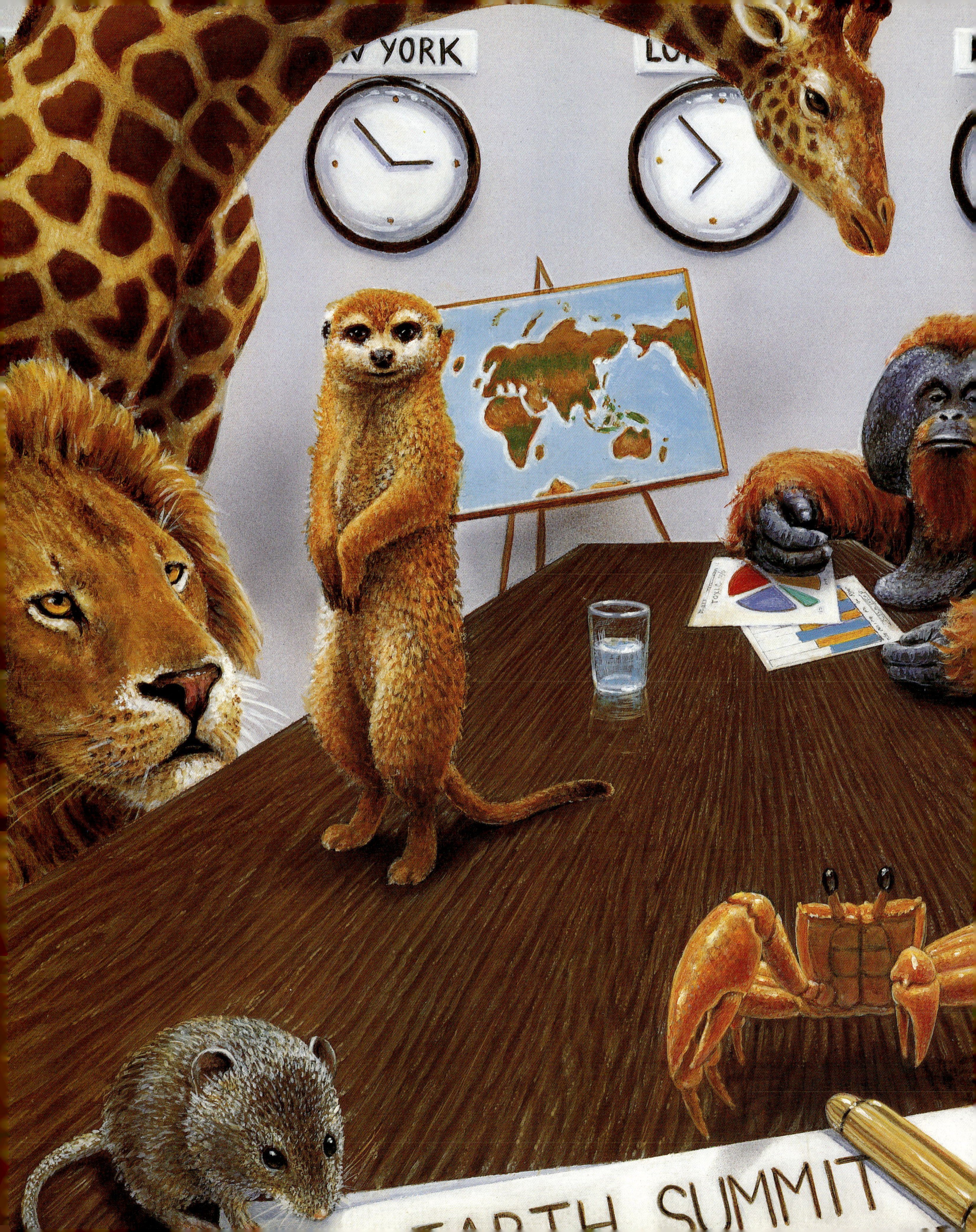
W YORK
SUMMIT

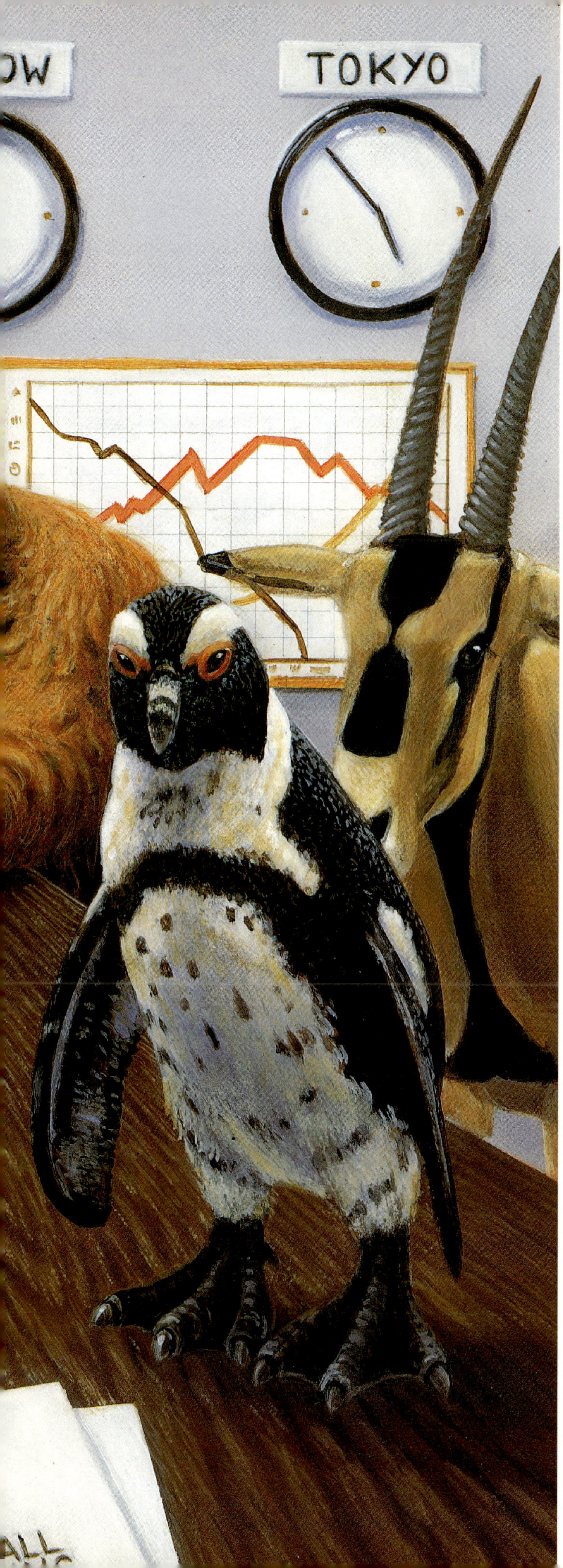

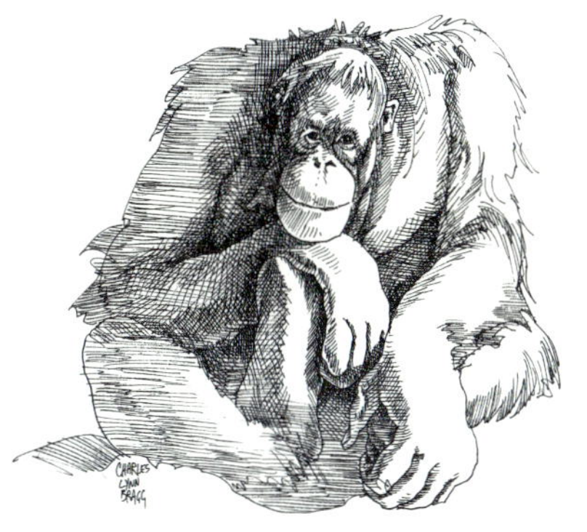

Orangutan

1990, acrylic on canvas, 14 x 18 in.

Corporate Takeover

1992, acrylic on canvas, 8 x 10 in.

I'd done a number of sketches. I thought about this one for a long time before I actually painted it. It's the corporate boardroom, where everything gets discussed and decided. The future of our world is decided in this boardroom, but these animals normally aren't there representing themselves or us. They don't usually get the choice to sign or not sign on the bottom line.

During the process, between when I sketched it and actually painted it, the 1992 Earth Summit was held in Rio. So this board meeting is the Earth Summit, and it's time to sign. They're all looking at us. The pen is there, waiting for us to pick it up and use it—giving everybody an equal chance here to survive.

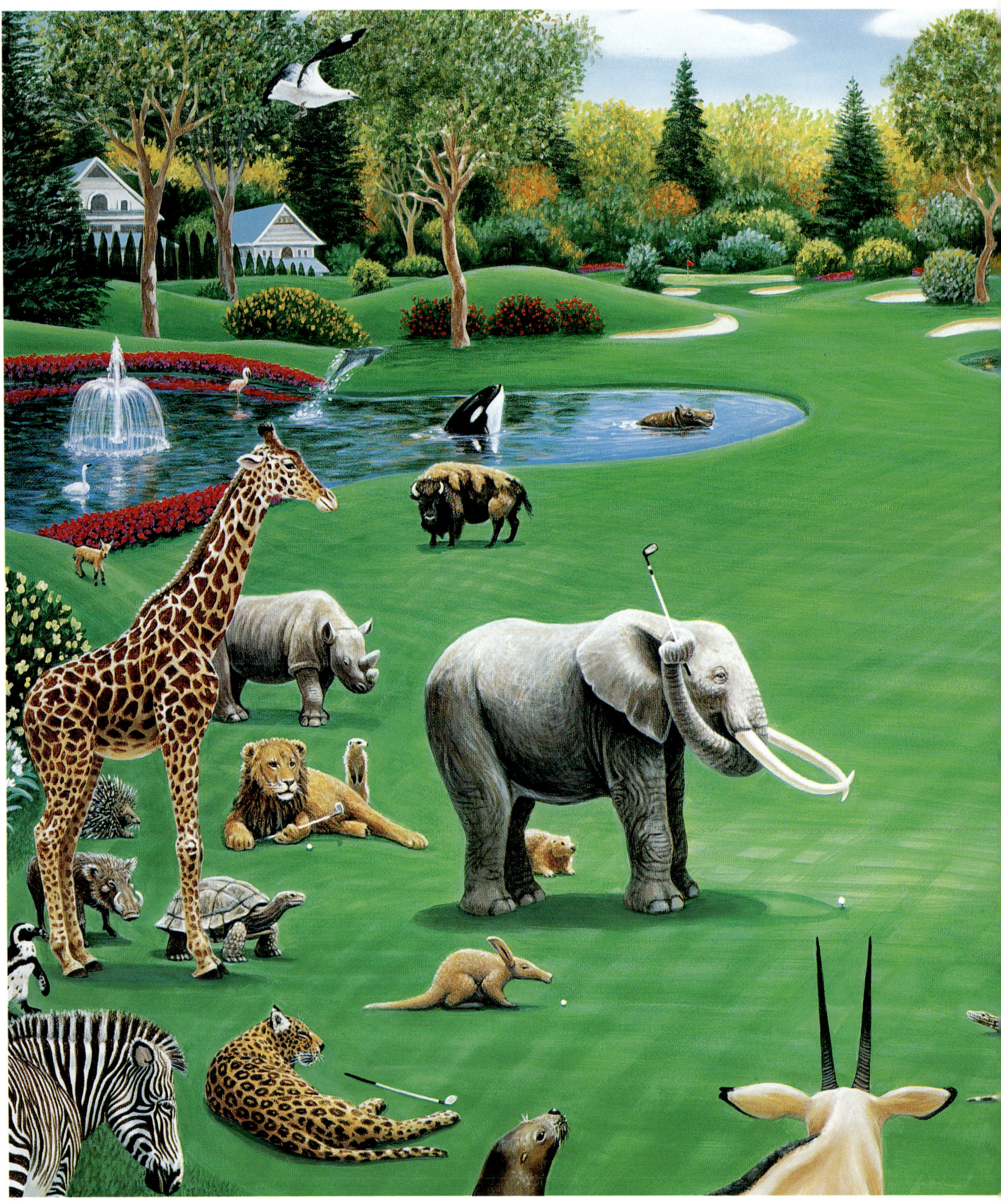

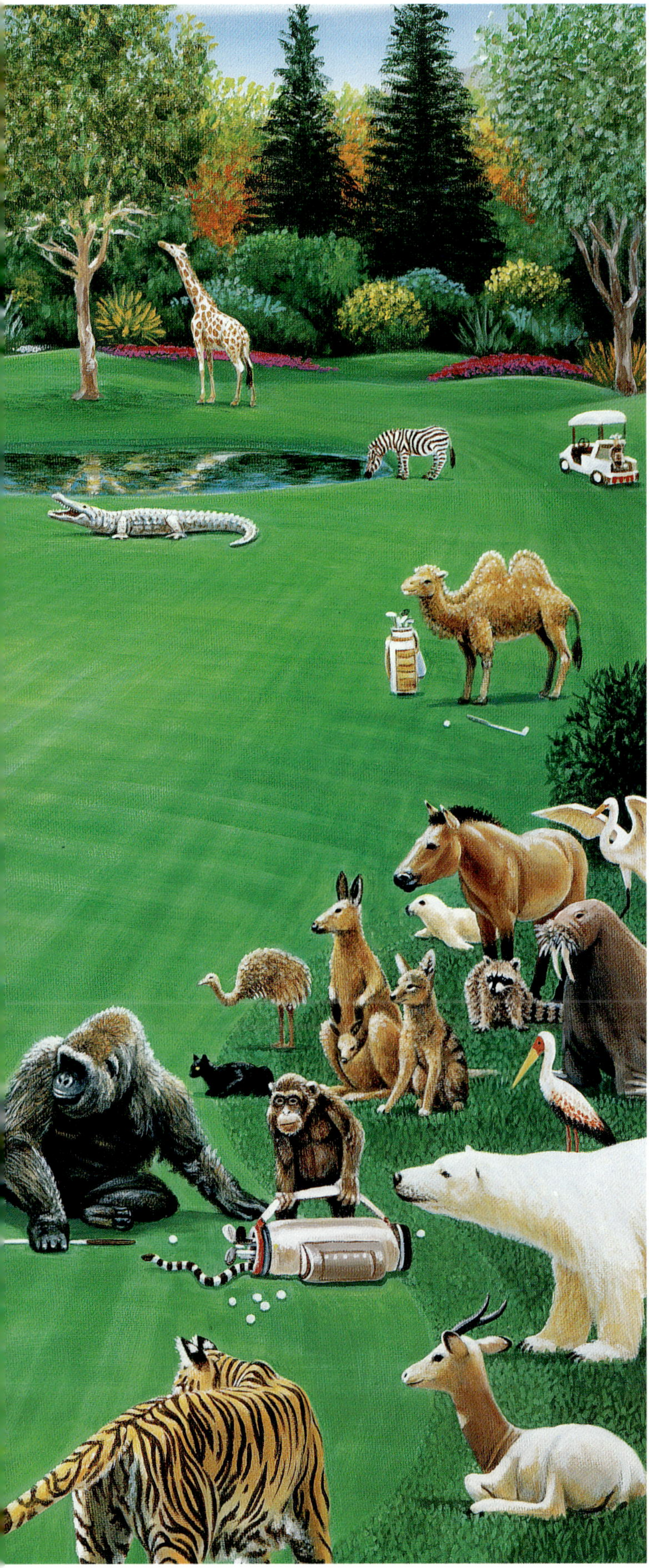

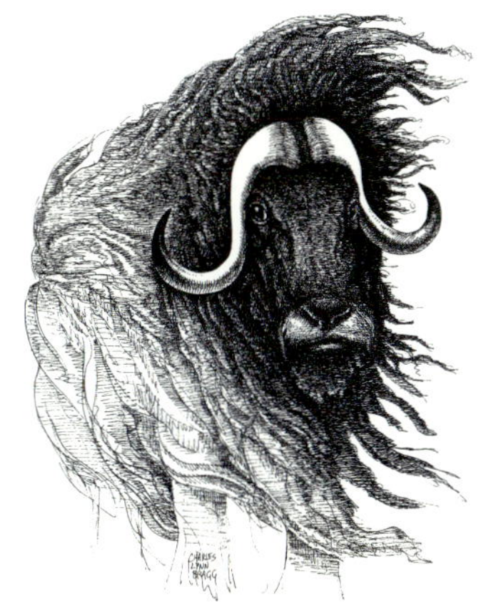

Dredlocks Musk Ox

1994, ink on paper, 12 x 11 in.

The Skins Game

1994, acrylic on canvas, 24 x 30 in.

I don't play golf, and I actually have a great concern for the animals that lose their homes and lives so that groups of human beings can go out and play a few rounds. Of course, I know many people like to play golf, and yes, some of my best friends are golfers. One couple I know decided to play at their local course on Valentine's Day in Margaret River, Western Australia. There are many resident kangaroos on that course—so many, in fact, that on this particular day, while my friends played, they watched in horror as rangers walked right up to the kangaroos and shot many of them in the head. For my golfing friends, Valentine's Day will never be the same. And so *The Skins Game* depicts the incongruity of animals playing at human games.

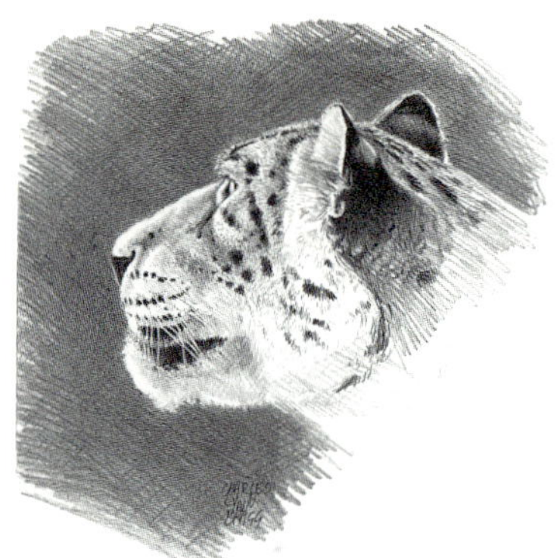

Snow Leopard

1994, pencil on paper, 8 x 8 in.

Red Jag

1993, acrylic on canvas, 8 x 10 in.

I had this beautiful photograph I took of a jaguar, and I had this nice little 8 by 10 canvas. I started painting him in there. He was on a white background. Then, I thought, he's got to be different somehow, so I put in this red background. When it was all red, I put this little square in here and filled it in with the jungle. I just pieced it together as I went along.

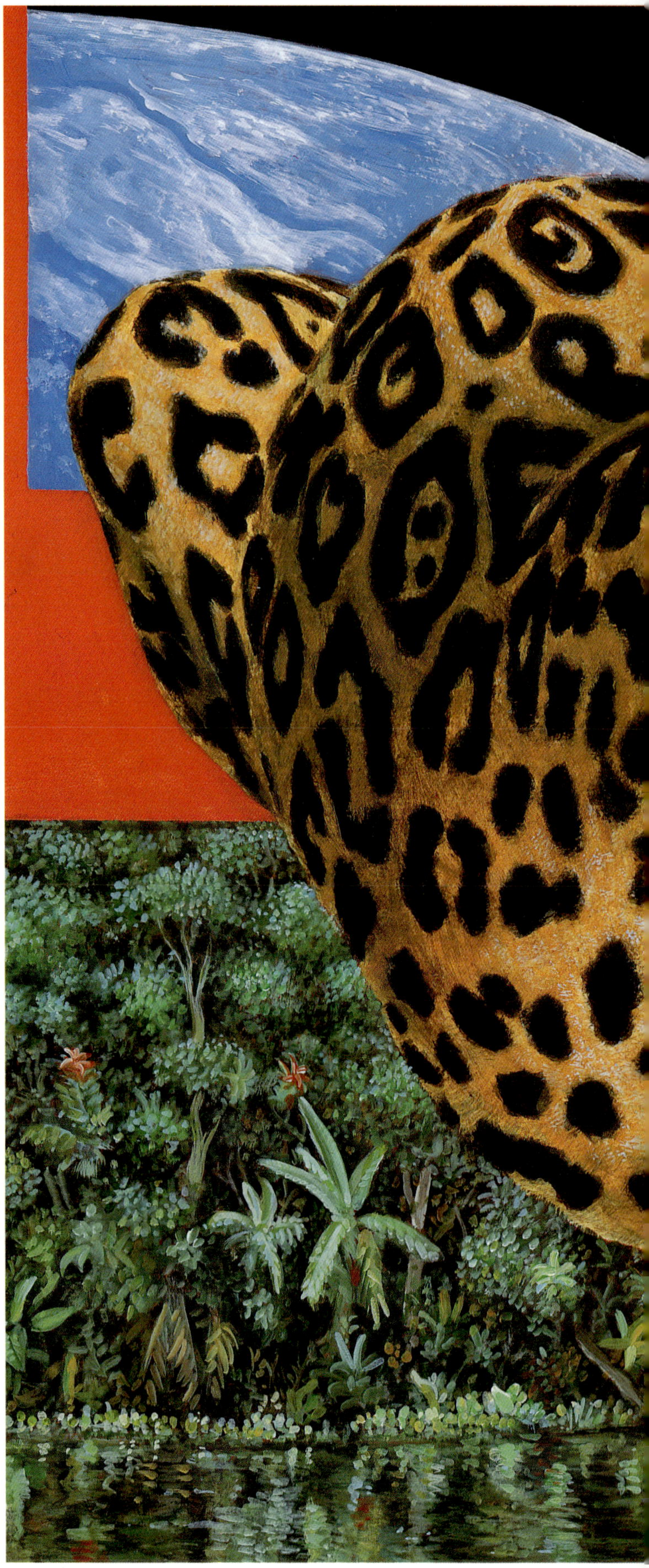

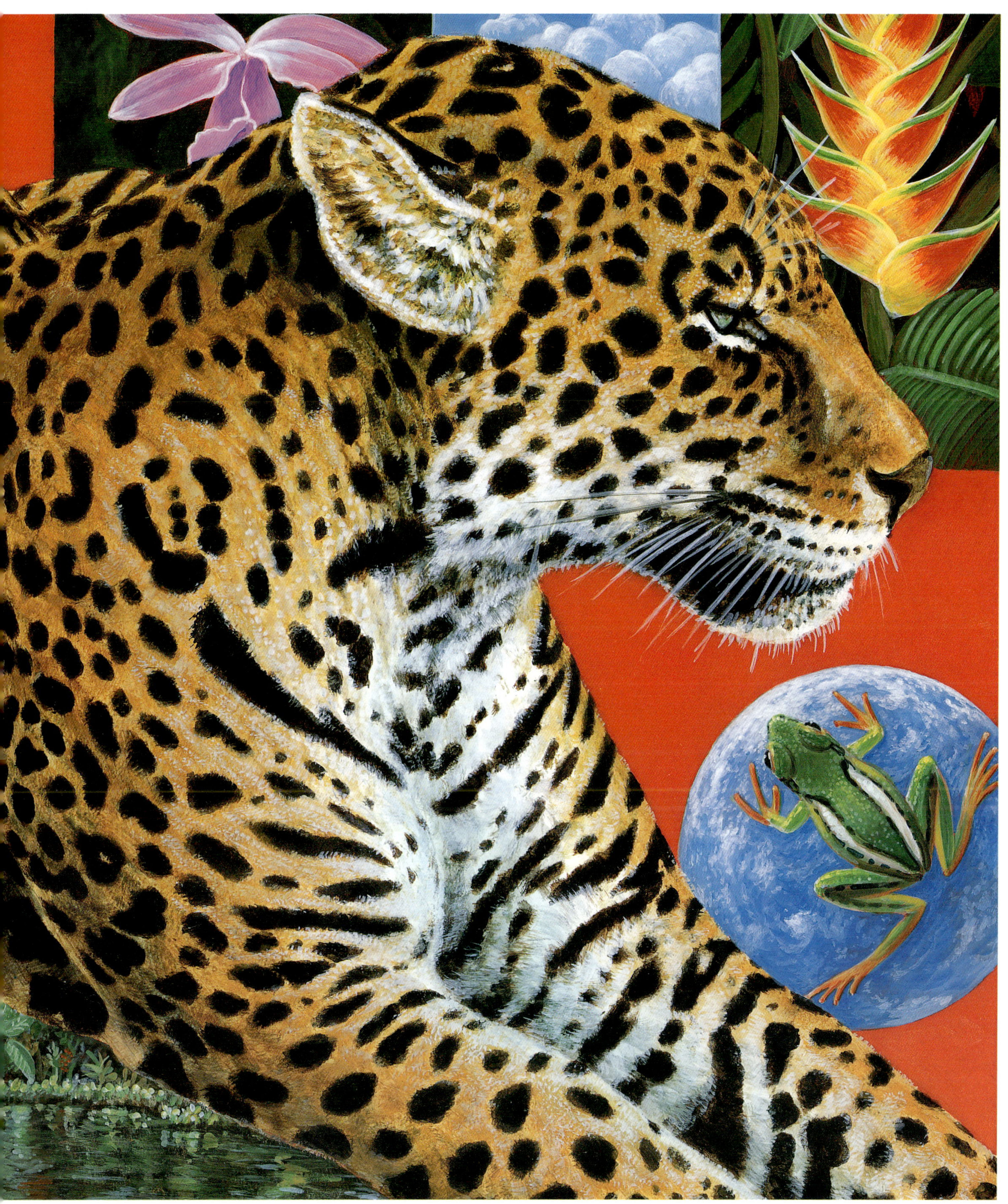

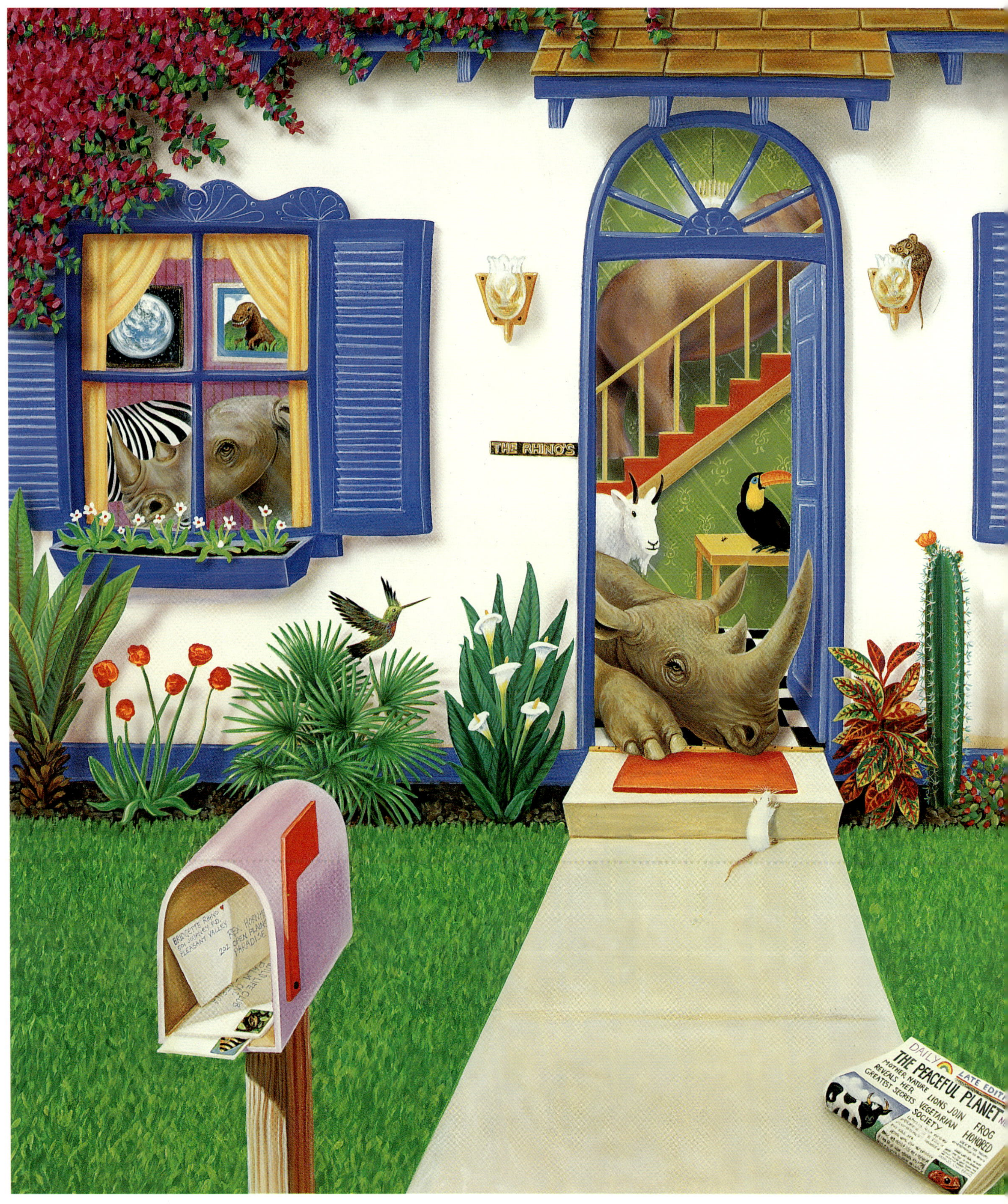
THE RHINO'S
BRIDGETTE RHINO
501 JOURNEY RD.
PLEASANT VALLEY
PARADISE
WILD LIFE CLUB
DAILY
THE PEACEFUL PLANET
LATE EDITI
MOTHER NATURE REVEALS HER GREATEST SECRETS
LIONS JOIN VEGETARIAN SOCIETY
FROG HONORED

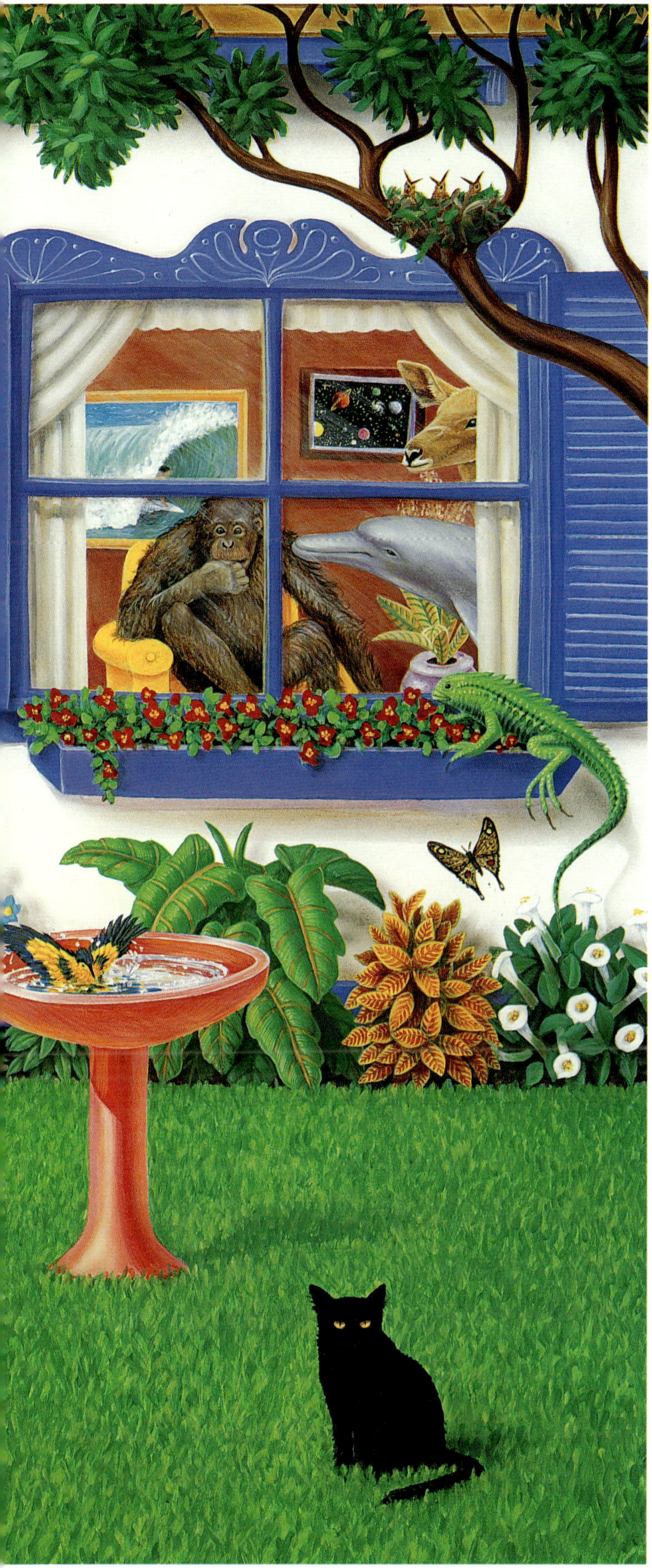

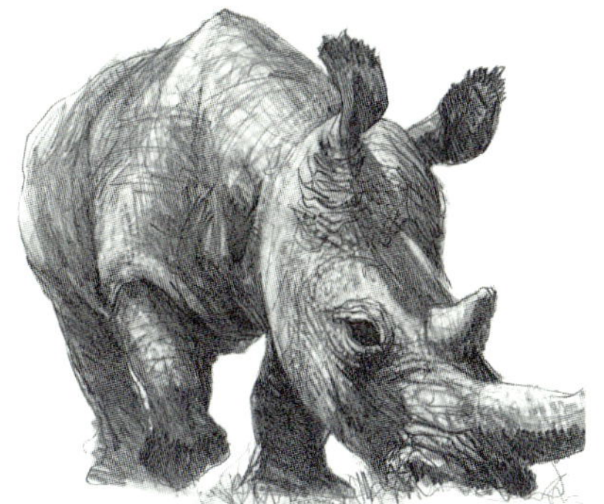

Rhinocerous

1983, pencil on paper, 14 x 15 in.

Animal House

1989, acrylic on canvas, 24 x 30 in.

This painting started a series of more whimsical pieces. The newspaper headlines say, "Mother Nature Reveals Her Greatest Secrets" alongside "Lions Join Vegetarian Society" and "Frog Honored."

I wanted it to be real colorful and primary and fun, almost cartoonish. I designed it with a ruler to get the edges straight and the structure of the house straight, because that's how things are. It was visually static and didn't excite me. So I gave subtle curves to all the lines. This makes it more animated. The doorway curves out. The walkway curves in. It wasn't something I planned. It was something where I said, "I don't know how to fix this image." So I just started curving the lines.

I was visiting a zoo in Morelia, Mexico, and in the zoo there was a big grass area with an adobe enclosure for the rhinos. It had a door and a roof, like a little house. A giant rhino was sitting, as if he were in the doorway of the house. It was perfect. The rhino's got an orangutan, a dolphin, and other friends over. A hippo is going upstairs—to powder her nose, perhaps.

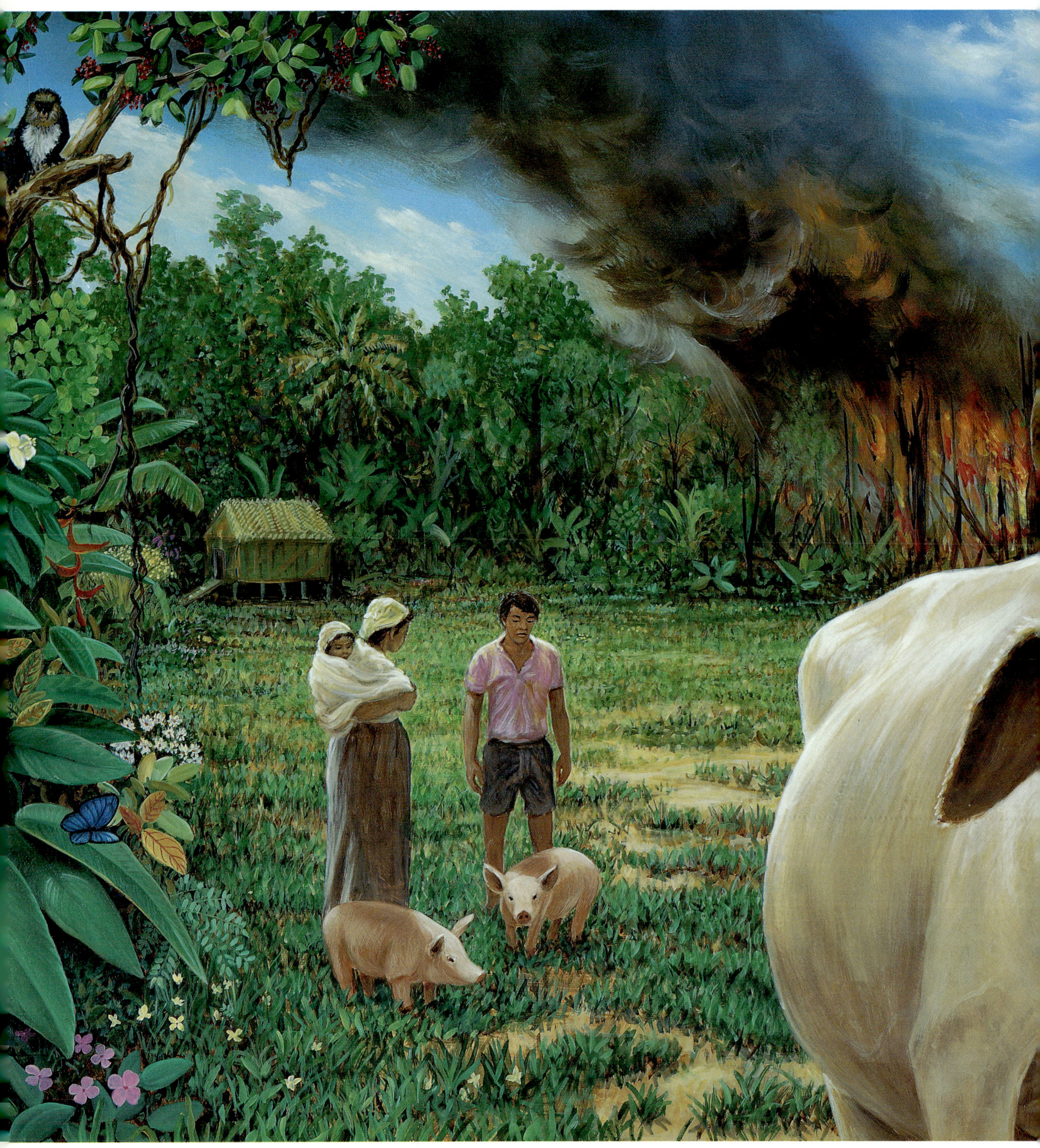

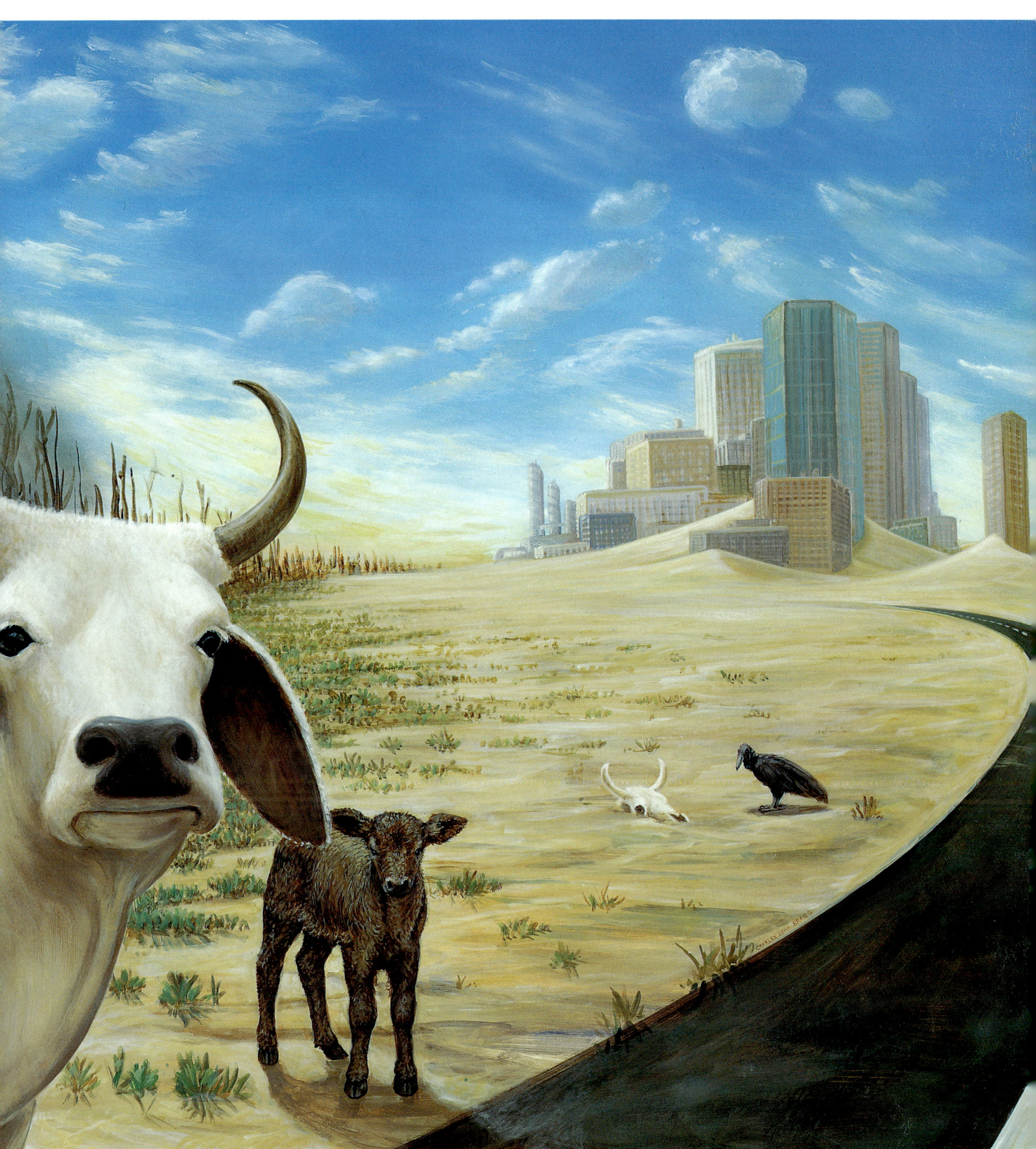
CHARLES LYNN BRAGG

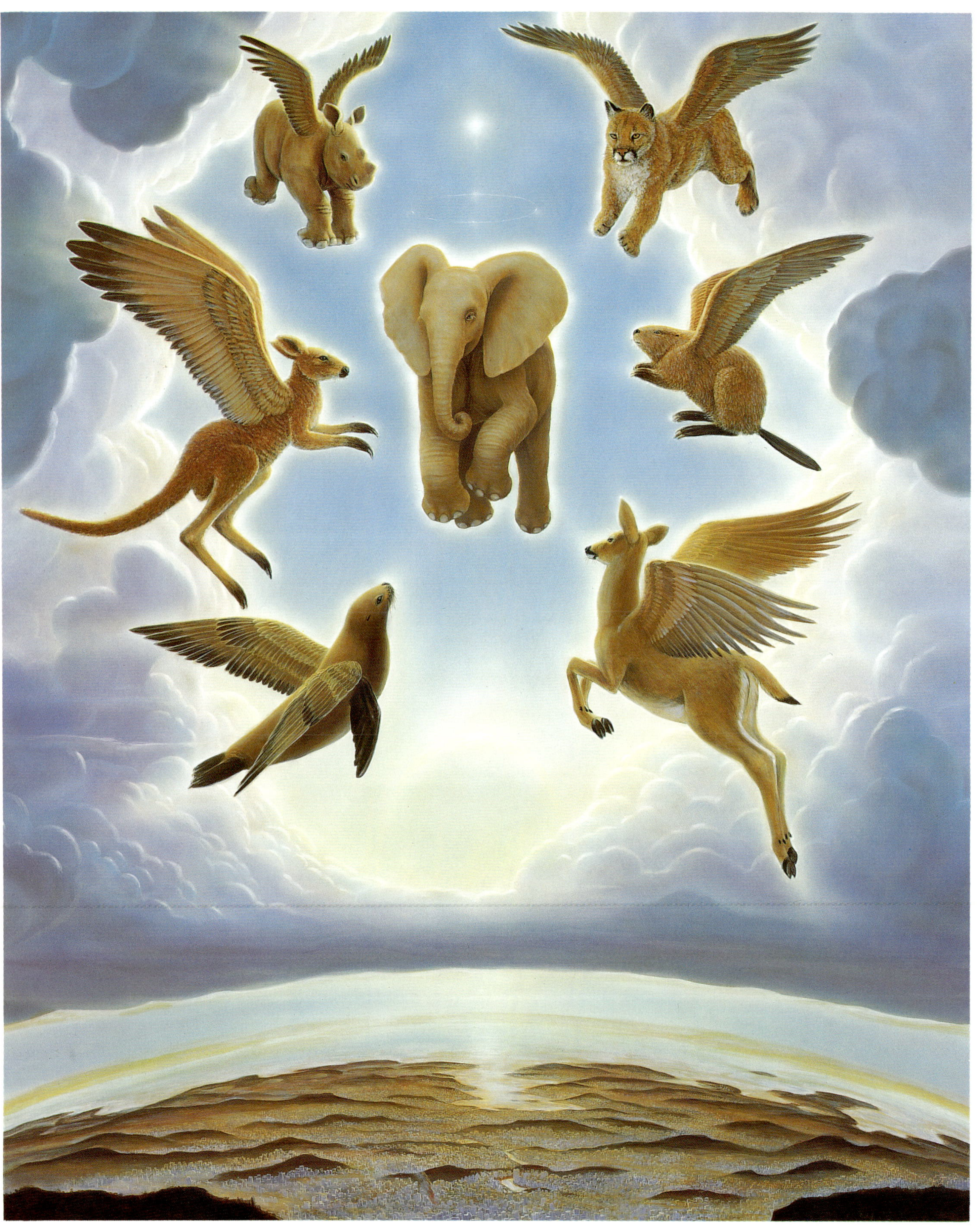

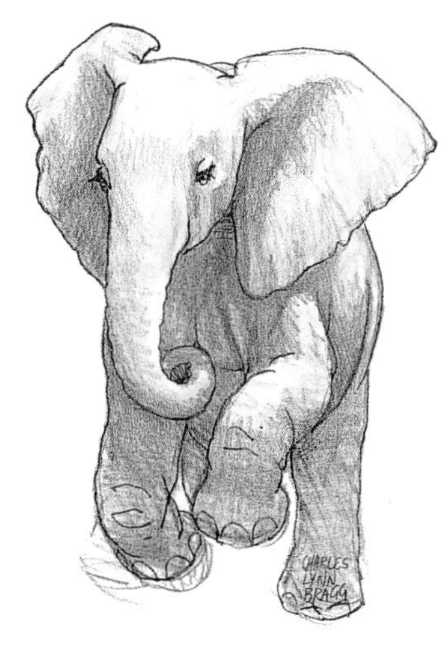

Dancing Elephant

1993, pencil on paper, 11 x 10 in.

The Last Supper

1990, acrylic on canvas, 18 x 36 in.
(Previous spread)

I went to Costa Rica to hike in the jungle and surf the waves. Deep in the jungle were primitive thatched huts and people subsisting along the little river. They live off the land. They grow bananas. They fish the river. Or they cut down forest and sell the wood for $300. They don't have TV. They don't get the nightly news. They don't see the global perspective. What they try to do is feed their families, and you really can't blame them. To cut down those five acres of rainforest is worthwhile for them. They can raise cattle. Of course, they don't realize that it will all turn into a desert if they keep cutting.

Heavenly Bodies

1992, acrylic on canvas, 30 x 24 in.
(Opposite)

I thought I would take an old theme from several hundred years ago, when the clouds open up and God comes through and does whatever he does. I found an old composition, with the earth at the bottom and the clouds and the horizon and the sky opening up. I thought: *In my heaven all the angels will be animals*. An elephant gets inducted into the Hall of Angels. He has just floated up on his way to get his wings. Down below, the earth is really small: a megalopolis, with smog and haze and skyscrapers that sprawl across every valley. While I was painting all these buildings, we had the riots here in L.A., so I added a little plume of fire.

We're losing all these beautiful creatures, and what are we replacing them with?

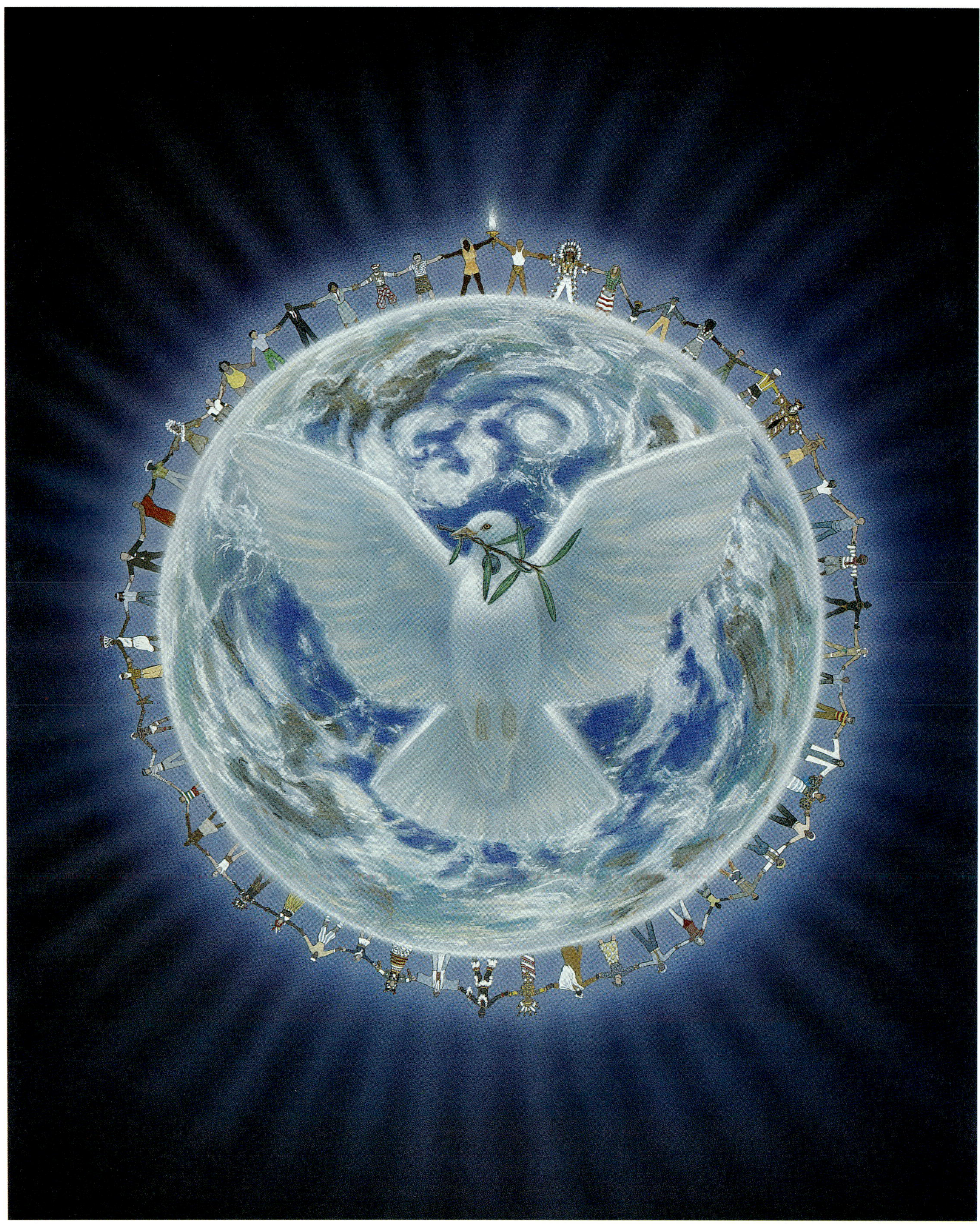

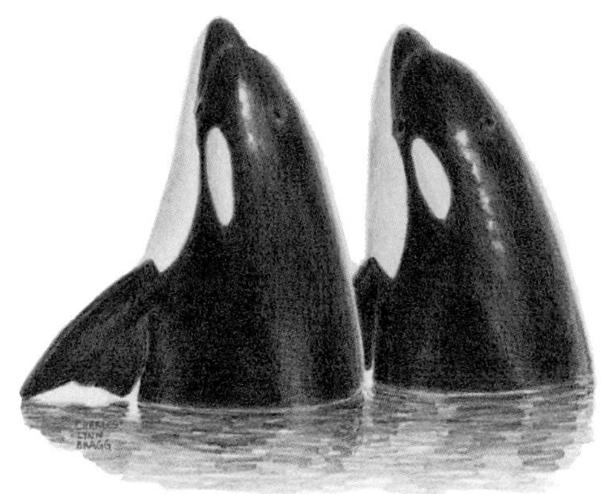

Two Orcas

1994, pencil on paper, 8 x 10 in.

Circle of Friends

1983, acrylic, ink and pastel on paper, 44 x 31 in.

In 1983, I think it was, a friend of mine was organizing a limited edition "good earth" promotion. The theme was the future of the planet. Well, I guess I didn't think much of our future. I drew a thumbnail sketch of a smoldering planet. But I looked at it, and I realized that I didn't want to project that kind of vision. Images are powerful, and I thought that by making a more optimistic image, we might have a better chance for a better world.

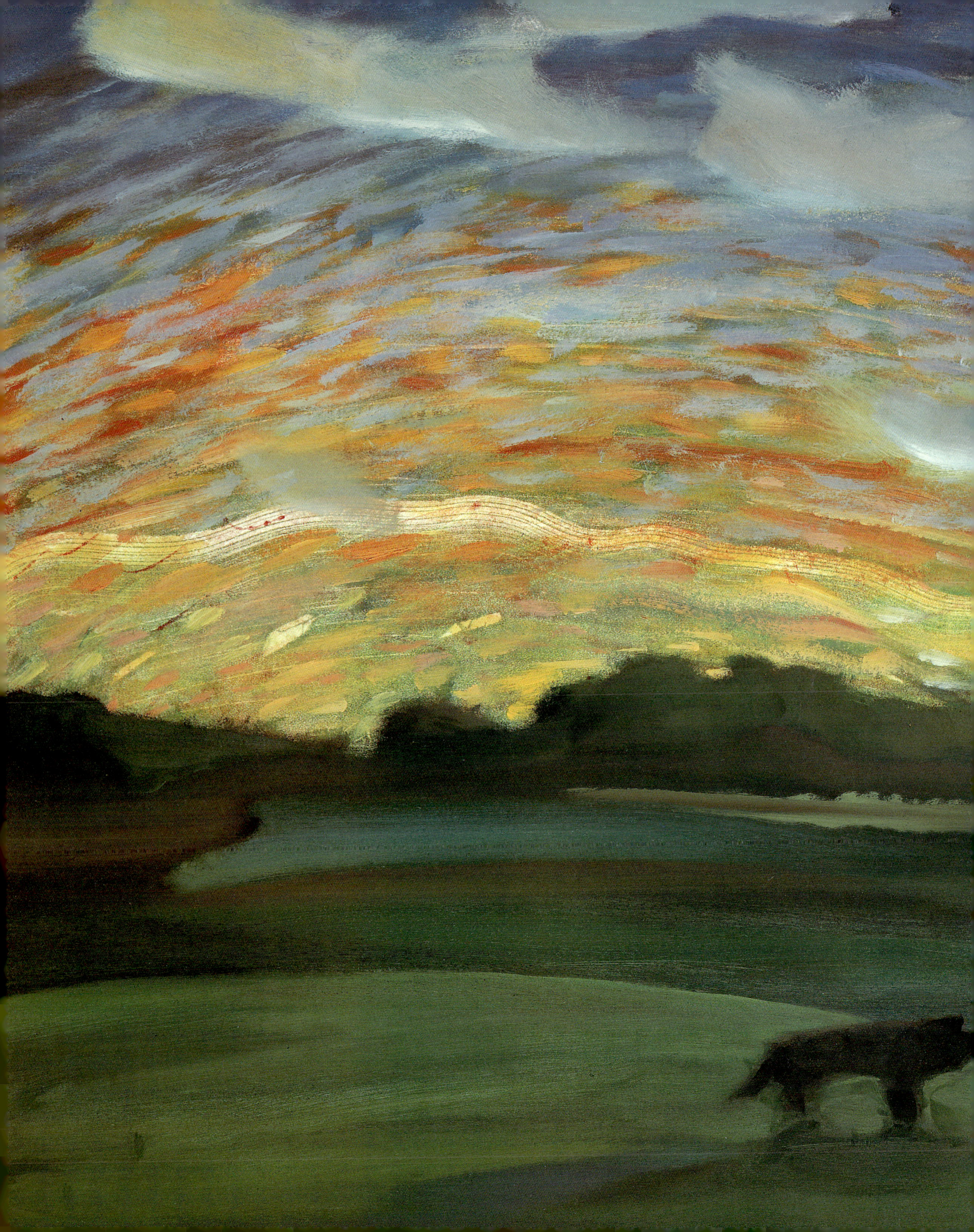

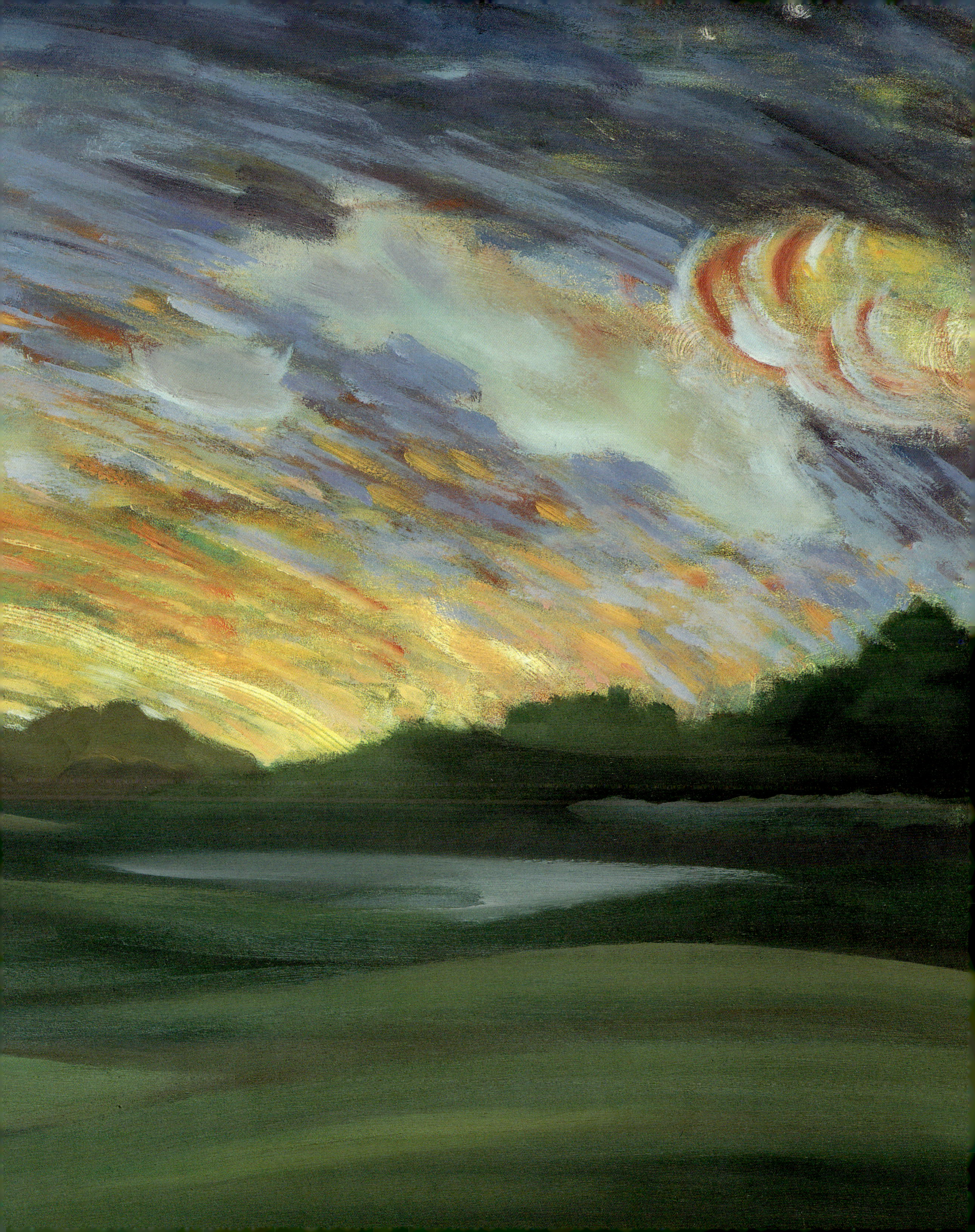

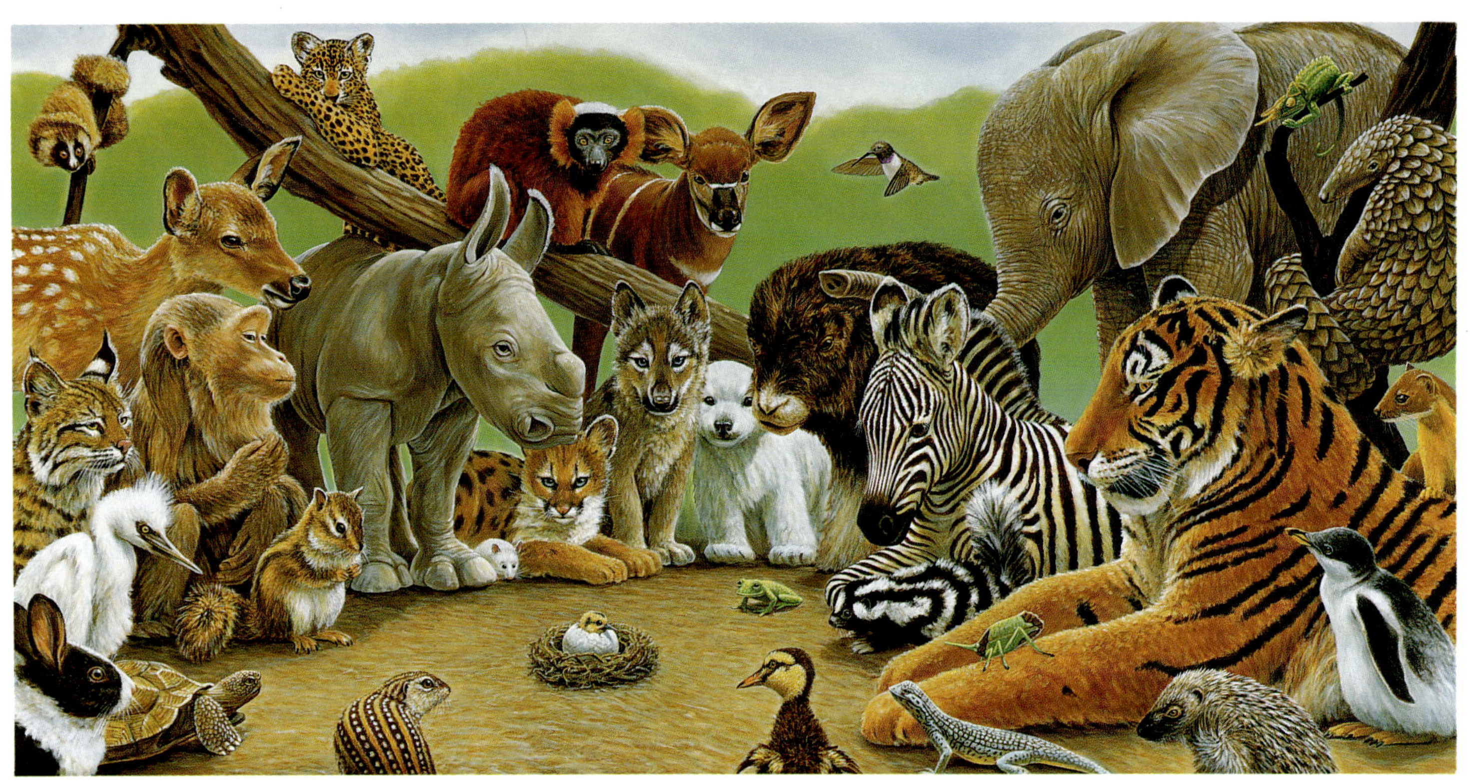

Little Miracle

1994, acrylic on canvas, 24 x 48 in.

I love the feeling I get from this painting: peaceful, patient, curious, transcendent, innocent, excited, focused on the miracle, the beauty and the promise of a new life being born on planet Earth.

Good-bye (Sarah)

1984, oil on paper, 18 x 24 in.

(Previous spread)

I made this painting for Sarah. Sarah was my dog, my best friend, my camping and hiking companion, and an all-around beach-loving, seagull-chasing mutt. We had many great adventures over her fourteen-year life, and when she died, she died in my arms. I have never cried so hard, and I am starting to get emotional now as I write. The painting depicts Sarah on her way to the "other side." She stops and takes one look back to say good-bye. I hope to see her again.